BLANKETS
AND
MOCCASINS

Plenty Coups, chief of all the tribes of the Northwest.

BLANKETS AND MOCCASINS

Plenty Coups and His People, the Crows

by Glendolin Damon Wagner
and Doctor William A. Allen

Foreword by Fred W. Voget

University of Nebraska Press
Lincoln and London

Copyright 1933 by The Caxton Printers, Ltd., Caldwell, Idaho
Foreword copyright 1987 by the University of Nebraska Press
All rights reserved
Manufactured in the United States of America

First Bison Book printing: 1987
Most recent printing indicated by the first digit below:
1 2 3 4 5 6 7 8 9 10

Library of Congress Cataloging-in-Publication Data
Wagner, Glendolin Damon.
Blankets and moccasins.
Reprint. Originally published: Caldwell, Idaho:
Caxton, 1933.
1. Crow Indians. 2. Plenty Coups, Chief of the
Crows, 1848–1932. 3. Allen, William Alonso, 1848–
4. Frontier and pioneer life — Montana. I. Allen,
William Alonzo, 1848– . II. Title.
E99.C92W24 1987   978.6'3'004970924 [B]   86-19316
ISBN 0-8032-4741-9
ISBN 0-8032-9713-0 (pbk.)

Reprinted by arrangement with The Caxton Printers, Ltd.

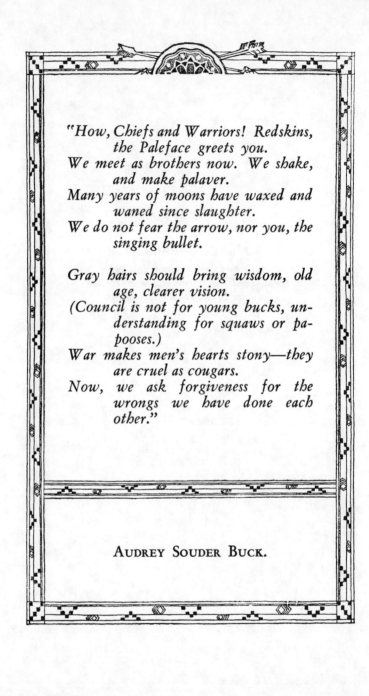

"How, Chiefs and Warriors! Redskins,
     the Paleface greets you.
We meet as brothers now. We shake,
     and make palaver.
Many years of moons have waxed and
     waned since slaughter.
We do not fear the arrow, nor you, the
     singing bullet.

Gray hairs should bring wisdom, old
     age, clearer vision.
(Council is not for young bucks, un-
     derstanding for squaws or pa-
     pooses.)
War makes men's hearts stony—they
     are cruel as cougars.
Now, we ask forgiveness for the
     wrongs we have done each
     other."

AUDREY SOUDER BUCK.

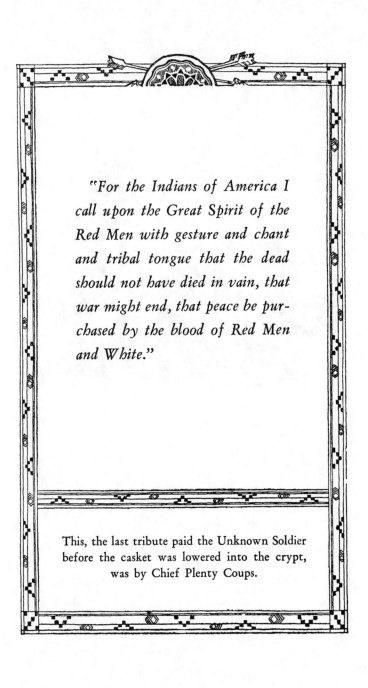

"For the Indians of America I call upon the Great Spirit of the Red Men with gesture and chant and tribal tongue that the dead should not have died in vain, that war might end, that peace be purchased by the blood of Red Men and White."

This, the last tribute paid the Unknown Soldier before the casket was lowered into the crypt, was by Chief Plenty Coups.

TABLE OF CONTENTS

LIST OF ILLUSTRATIONS

FOREWORD
by Fred W. Voget

Blankets and Moccasins is high adventure in the western style. It is based on the personal reminiscences of Ohio-born "Doc" Bill Allen, who came to Crow Indian country in Montana when these proud hunters and warriors were being forced into a restless and ambiguous life on a government-run reservation. Life on a reservation without buffalo hunts and warrior raids for horses were all part of the taming of the West. Indeed, Doc Allen himself, in his manifold careers as hunter, goldseeker, blacksmith at Fort Custer, and then dentist in Billings, Montana, reflected changes that were turning the Old West into memories and reminiscences.

High adventure and superficial descriptions of Indian character and custom are typical of western adventures with Indians. However, *Blankets and Moccasins* is an exception, despite western stereotypic references to "buck," "squaw," and "pagan."

Two special experiences took Allen beyond the usual limited understandings of those who fought Indians and those who later came to teach "civilization." His first and most important experience occurred shortly after the defeat of Custer at the Battle of the Little Big Horn. It was a confrontation with Plenty Coups, a chief of the Crows. Allen was in charge of a gold-seeking wagon train, and before they made camp along the Little Big Horn River, they met up with Plenty Coups and twenty of his warriors. No explanation of friendly purpose or invitation to share elk and buffalo meat could dispel the aloof suspicion of Plenty Coups. As preparations for the meal brought tantalizing aromas of "wood smoke and sizzling steak and boiling coffee" drifting past Crow nostrils, friendship in true western fashion began with good eating and a sociable building of trust. When Allen generously gave five needle guns recently taken from the Sioux to Plenty Coups, and spontaneously pledged to assist the Crows against the Sioux, he found himself swearing by the steel blade of a knife to be their friend until death. A pledge to stand together against a common enemy, the Sioux, thus tightened the sinews of friendship between white and Indian.

Allen's second experience was a rescue mission. During a November blizzard in 1879, Allen became aware of people milling aimlessly about in the snow about a mile away from his ranch house. When he reached them, he recognized Chief Pretty Eagle, his wife, and daughter. Somehow he managed to get them astride their tired ponies and brought them to the warm fire of his ranch home. There Allen and his wife revived the near frozen chief and family.

Friendship leveled cultural barriers between Crow and white, and as these two chiefs in gratitude opened their hearts and lives to him, Allen got an inside view of "Indian character." The bond with Plenty Coups grew especially close and Doc Allen learned how Crows, in their struggle against their enemies, substituted courage for fear. Mothers took over the early training, pampering their newborn laced in the cradle. But in his memories of early childhood Plenty Coups must have shivered as he recalled how his mother plunged him daily into icy waters to build his tolerance for cold. She also sent him into the dark of night for wood, and if he returned afraid, she sent him off again. Crow warriors ever stood guard over camp and family, and from his mother's lullabies, Plenty Coups remembered the inspiring words "Every day be strong and brave and make the enemy run. Got to be a man and brave." When things went wrong, it was not the sting of whip or stick that kept him in line, but ridicule.

The Crows occupied a homeland rich in buffalo and they were favored middlemen in the trade in horses between the Shoshonis, from whom they obtained their horses, and the village-dwelling Mandans and Hidatsas living beside the Missouri River in North Dakota. The Crows were proud traders and became noted for their quality tipis, equipment, and horses. They were a preferred target for horse-raiding Sioux, Cheyennes, Arapahos, and Piegans. The Crows needed to be superb warriors, for their population of six to eight thousand was no match for their enemies. Accepting challenges and competing with a sense of pride in self and in family were essential to Crow training in personal success and to tribal survival. Boys raced, swam, rode, and hunted in competition just as warriors competed in war honors. Praise and ridicule were the carrot and stick of Crow training, which idealized the warrior-leader blessed with a supernatural power granted by spirit-persons, the "medicine fathers." They knew that nothing succeeds like success, and in the competitive world Plenty Coups faced, his mother, perceiving that he had less speed and more endurance for racing than his boyhood rivals, extended the distance so he could win.

A warrior's life bonded man with man, and beyond a mother's care, the Crows relied on an older brother to guide a younger. At five years of age, Plenty Coups sneaked away in the early dawn with his ten-year-old brother to hunt rabbits, or the two of them floated down the Little Big Horn in a bull boat their mother had built for their explorations. In the years ahead Plenty Coups could count on his maternal uncles, who also in Crow usage were "older brothers," to help him learn a warrior's skills.

As a teenage youth, Plenty Coups's brother turned the corner to manhood, and in solitary fast under wise guidance sought out a "medicine-father" to bestow on him the mystic power so essential to success as a warrior and in life generally. The older brother undoubtedly joined peers organized as a military fraternity modeled after the Kit-Foxes or Lumpwoods of mature warriors. The older now had no time for his younger brother and Plenty Coups found it hard to accept this separation, for some of the excitement and fresh learning had gone out of his life. Then one day his brother went out on a raid to recover Crow horses and was killed by the Sioux. From that time forward Plenty Coups lived to fulfill a vow of revenge. His every move was a preparation for that vengeful triumph, but even as he succeeded in that vow, the coup was but the beginning of his career. He had earlier determined to become head chief of the Crows and he never swerved from that purpose, even after it became a reality. He had committed himself to be a winner in everything, and winner he was.

The Indian men Doc Allen came to know in friendship were quite different from the popular stereotype. They were grateful for favors received, staunchly loyal and kind in friendship, courageous and competitively ambitious for public honors, but throughout it all they were proud but not arrogant. True, when with whites, they maintained a dignified aloofness, but then they knew not what to expect. Crow men and women appreciated family life and enjoyed their children, who seemed to hold center stage. It was not just that parents did their utmost to satisfy childhood wants and complaints. Crow society was so structured that both parents and their relatives cooperated so that a child succeeded in life. A Crow traced his lineage through his mother and belonged to his mother's clan. However, a father's clansmen were very important to a boy, for he was their "child" and they were his clan "fathers." Through their medicine dreams, clan "fathers" and "mothers" kept their "child" free of sickness and danger from season to season. As he grew to manhood clan "fathers" gave a "child" medicine dreams which directed him to successes over the enemy. In return a "child" and his mother's clan relatives gave horses, buffalo robes, and other good things, usually distributed at a feast to which the father's clansmen were invited.

Doc Allen had another facet in his experiences that touched the sensitive relations between the Crow and whites during the transition to reservation life. These experiences centered in the running down of horse raiders and in the gambling and partying that went on at Hoskin and McGirl's trading post situated on the present site of Huntley, Montana.

It was a September day in 1880 that Doc Allen joined a war party led by Plenty Coups in pursuit of Blackfeet who had run off some twenty horses. Allen was a willing partner, for he too had lost six head. In this time of power transition from Indian chief to Indian agent, Plenty Coups was shrewd enough to know that having whites along in such a chase was good politics. They caught up with the Blackfeet party, and in the hand-to-hand combats which ensued, Doc Allen found himself pinned to the ground and expected his end had come. But suddenly the Blackfeet "giant" collapsed and "there was Plenty Coups, war club in hand, smiling his calm smile." Now it was Allen's turn to acknowledge that he owed his life to a Crow Indian, his friend, sworn on the oath with the blade of a knife.

After the serious trading of hides and horses for calicoes, beads, guns, powder, and other goods, Crow and white trappers at the Hoskin and McGirl's post were ready for some gambling fun. They usually worked up to it with a rousing buffalo barbecue backed with plenty of whiskey chasers. They pledged greenbacks, blankets, hides, horses, and shirts off their backs. There was no time in playing horseshoes to wait for the end of the game, so Crows bet against whites individually with each throw. When the pleasure of horseshoes ran out, someone always thought of target shooting—at beer bottles, a spot on a distant cliff for sharpshooting, and then precision shooting at twenty yards or so. With so much good fun there always was a time and place for a showdown between Crow and white, especially when a Crow Indian and a white man laid claim to the same horse. On one spring day in 1879, though, all the good-natured camaraderie vanished and Plenty Coups arrived just in time to mediate and stop a fracas. He held in favor of the white man since the horse carried that man's brand and the Crow had no paper to show that he had purchased the horse as claimed. It was a time of show-down with the Crow Indian, by the name of Snow, who gave up the horse at Plenty Coups's direction.

In those twilight days when the Crows were still par-tially mobile, hunting the last of the buffalo and visit-ing posts for trade, horse racing between Indians and whites was a prime pastime and gambling event. There is no better description of what went on at these racing events than the "Last Great Horse Race of the North-west."

The Crows had always been friendly to whites, even

when gaining a reputation for their skill at running off
the horses of pack trains and other emigrant Yellow
Eyes, as they called the whites. However, the loss of
their buffalo-hunting and raiding life was not easy to
accept. In 1887 a young Crow by the name of Wraps-
Up-His-Tail chafed under the restraints imposed by the
agent and the soldiers. In a fast in the mountains he had
been given a power that made him invincible, for soldiers would fall like leaves when he sang his medicine
song and pointed the sword. Thus he became known as
Sword-bearer and he and his youthful followers aroused
anxious fears of a Crow "insurrection." Doc Allen's
views of this episode were quite contrary to a popular
feeling voiced in the *Billings Gazette.* In an editorial the
Gazette asserted that Indians must be forced to submit
and made to understand "that to become like a whiteman is their only hope to escape utter annihilation." In
Allen's opinion "the whole trouble developed because
the young Crow agitator, Sword-bearer, had become
very like the whiteman in his political shrewdness, his
vanity and ambition and greed." Most of the blame for
this unfortunate and unnecessary affair fell squarely
upon Agent H. E. Williamson, whose prior actions had
aroused the hatred of the Crow, and the attempt to
arrest Sword-bearer and his followers after a horse raid
simply compounded the mismanagement of his office.

Blankets and Moccasins made its appearance fifty-six
years after the Sword-bearer episode. In Billings and
Sheridan, towns not far from the Crow Reservation, res-
taurants still denigrated Indians and most refused to

serve them. Allen wanted people to know that "young
Indians starting out in life must contend against racial
competition as well." Indians often were "bewildered
victims of so many bungling experiments," and one lesson they learned over and over again was that the white
man's might made right. Most Crows sensed that in the
exchange of the hunter's life for civilization they were
the losers. Under the hunter's life, with all its hardships
and warring hazards, they were free and provided for
themselves.

Like most frontier narrators of experiences with Indians, Doc Allen is not one to probe the details and mean-
ings of Crow customs. Ethnographic errors are mini-
mal, but on page 146, the reference to the Sun Dance
actually is to a Scalp Dance, and Plains Indians did not
use "poisoned" arrows. The date of 350 "winters" ago
given for the combination of tribes to attack the Crow,
as narrated by Chief Pretty Eagle, is hardly accurate.

Even though *Blankets and Moccasins* may not contain
the ethnographic detail of some personal narratives of
Plains Indians, Doc Allen and his coauthor, Glendolin
Wagner, have succeeded in merging the excitement of
western adventure with rich insights into Crow Indian
life and character. The descriptions of Crow-White relations during the transition to reservation life present
important material not found in narratives of the buffalo-hunting days.

Blizzard on Cañon Creek

(Excerpt from Dr. Allen's Journal.)

NOVEMBER 22, 1879 — Here it is almost Thanksgiving! Well, we've got a lot to be thankful for this year. A good roof over our heads—a shingled roof, at that—the only one in the valley—a barrel of flour and one of sugar, enough dried elk meat and frozen buffalo to last us through the winter, hay in the corral so Prince won't have to forage over snow-covered plains unless he wants to, and timber on the hills to keep our fires roaring a thousand years.

Yesterday Mother said she wished she could have a little fresh meat for a change, so this afternoon Willie and I are going rabbit hunting. A hot rabbit stew with plenty of gravy for supper won't taste so bad.

November 23—Yesterday Willie and I went onto the hills back of the house after rabbits. We got four and saw an antelope but too far away for a shot. The snow was waist deep on the plains and up to my neck in the coulees. I never saw so much snow in Montana. All day yesterday it fell, and all last night, and is still coming down.

November 24—Still snowing. Flakes coming straight down, as big as pop corn and light as feathers. Colder today. I'm going to hitch Prince to some logs and haul them up against the house. No telling how long this spell's going to last.

November 27—Had a regular blizzard yesterday. All of a sudden the wind began blowing and came roaring down Cañon Creek with the force of a tornado, piling snow sky high and filling the air with nettles of ice that cut into the flesh. When I bundled up and started out to the corral for Prince to go after some logs Mother begged me not to. She said she'd read of men getting lost in blizzards like this just going from the house to the barn. As I opened the door and let in raging gusts of icy wind that stung and smothered I decided she was right. I gave up the idea of going after logs but thought I'd better go out to the corral and see how the animals were making it.

Closing the door behind me I looked through the storm and thought I saw, down the valley, at the foot of a butte, a speck darker than surrounding whiteness—a speck that moved. Probably some buffalo, I thought, huddled against the storm.

But there was a possibility it might be my horses the Blackfeet had stolen the week before, broken loose and trying to get back home. So I rushed into the house for my field glasses and climbed to the platform I had built as a lookout on the roof of our cabin. From there I could see that the moving speck was neither buffalo nor horses but human beings wrapped in blankets and milling about aimlessly through deep snow.

I leaped down from the roof and rushed into the house. "Keep the fire going full blast," I shouted. "Have plenty of hot water ready. Make coffee. There's folks lost down by the butte and I'm going after them."

Prince and I went floundering through drifts, down into hidden coulees and up again, stumbling over snow-covered logs at the risk of our necks. A long, hard mile, but we made it. It was folks, all right, but, by the time I got to them, they weren't moving. They had fallen down into a deep ravine and were lying still, almost buried in snow. I could tell by their blankets they were Indians—a man and his squaw and child. Around a bend where I hadn't seen them from my lookout were two ponies, tired out, standing backs to the storm, with heads drooping.

I let out a loud "How!" but there was no response, no slightest stir of the motionless figures in the snow. I jumped off Prince and seized the big buck by the shoulder and shook him. He grunted an indignant protest and opened sleep-glazed eyes and closed them again. He was in the last stages of freezing and was numbed past suffering and wanted nothing so much, now, as to be left alone.

I shook him again but couldn't wake him up. I pounded with my fists and kicked him with my heavy boots and he just grunted wearily and kept on sleeping. Then I measured him with my eye— a big hulk of a man, broad of shoulder and all of six feet tall. I'm not a dwarf myself, but to manage his dead weight was out of the question. So I kept on smacking his face and punching his ribs until I made him good and mad. He struggled to his feet, shaking off the deadening inertia, and I pointed to his squaw and papoose lying quiet in the snow.

That brought him to his senses. Together he and I loaded the woman and child onto a pony. With my help he climbed onto his and sagged there, hands nerveless, head nodding, drifting off to sleep again. In that half-dead condition nobody but an Indian could have stuck to his horse. I grabbed up the rawhide ropes of his horses, took a half-hitch around my saddle horn, got onto Prince, and started for the house, following the trail I'd made coming out. I thought we'd never get there. Twice the squaw slipped from her horse and had to be lifted on again, and the buck couldn't help me. My own hands and feet were aching cruelly. Never in my life has anything looked so good to me as the rosy glow of fire shining through the windows of my cabin.

First I lifted the child from the pony and carried her into the house and placed her in my wife's outstretched arms. I know of no better haven for a suffering child than those arms. The squaw came next. I laid her on the floor in front of the fireplace and went back for the big Indian. He was a load, leaning on me so heavily, stumbling along on frosted feet, but I managed him.

Quickly my wife and I stripped the Indians of their buffalo coats and leggins. We brought pans of snow and rubbed frozen hands and feet and faces—worked over them at least an hour before they began showing signs of life. At last the man sat up and stared at me, eyes bleared in his swollen face, and I recognized Pretty Eagle, a Crow chief.

"How!" I said, but he did not answer.

My wife brought in steaming cups of coffee. He took one in eager hands but did not drink until he made sure his squaw was being as kindly treated. She was sitting up now, still numbed and dazed, though quite out of danger. Their little papoose, a girl of six, was already running about the room, gazing curiously at all the odd furnishings of a white man's tepee, smiling at our son Willie, and using feminine wiles to make friends with him.

Then, while our guests were sitting cross-legged on the floor, drowsy and comfortable, and while Mother was flying about in the kitchen I went out into the storm once more to lead the tired, shivering Indian ponies into the corral where there was shelter for them and water and plenty of hay.

When I got back the kitchen was filled with the smell of delicious food. Mother had the table set and steaming dishes on it—coffee and potatoes and buffalo tongues and boiled cabbage and even a dried raspberry pie right out of the oven, its rich, syrupy juice oozing through the crust. My wife had done herself proud. And what a feast we had! We all sat around the table, silent at first, intent upon the important business of eating as much as we could possibly hold. Those Indians seemed famished.

At last, after Pretty Eagle with unquestionable relish had consumed the last flaky crumb of his pie, he looked at me across the table, studied my face gravely. He shaded his snow-blinded eyes with a hand and peered at me. Then he got up slowly and came to me and placed an arm about my shoulders.

"White Eagle?" he inquired.

I nodded and smiled. "Yes," I said, "that's the name you gave me—you and Plenty Coups—the time I killed the big white bear up in the Pryors."

"White Eagle," he repeated, "white brother of the Crows. Today you saved our lives."

He was deeply moved. It is given few white men to witness an Indian brave shedding tears, but I swear at that moment his eyes were misted with tears—tears of gratitude. When he spoke his voice was husky.

"White Eagle saved my life," he remarked,

Mrs. Wagner with Dr. Allen on Indian mound in Pryor Pass. (In background is the cañon where Crows awaited enemies' attack. Chief Pretty Eagle's story of the battle fought 350 years ago.)

solemnly. "Saved the life of my squaw and my little meercotty. White Eagle heap brave man. Indian never forgets kindness."

"Oh, pshaw, that was nothing!" I said.

He was silent for a time, thinking. Then he went on in his slow, solemn voice: "Many snows have fallen upon my head. My father was one hundred and eight years old when he died, his father more than that. Now, because you saved my life and my heart sings I will tell you a secret my father's father told to him and he told to me— a secret no white man knows, and few living Crows. So are secrets kept in our tribe without writing, and remembered.

"Our young men no longer listen to the stories of the old ones. They do not tell their sons. Soon the history of our tribe will be lost forever—history written in blood. So today Pretty Eagle will tell to White Eagle, the brother of the Crows, the secret history of our tribe. He will write it in the book of the palefaces so Crow boys may read and remember. Today, because he saved my life and the life of my squaw and little meercotty he shall learn what no white man knows—learn what is in those mounds in the valley along Pryor Creek."

I was very much interested. I shoved back my chair. "Come to the fire," I said.

We all sat down on the floor, cross-legged, in front of the fireplace. I filled a pipe and lit it and handed it to Pretty Eagle. I filled another for myself. Without speaking we sat and smoked and looked into the flames the way Indians like to do.

For so long a time the Indian remained silent I thought he'd forgotten his promise or that his words had been spoken in idle jest. I, who know the Indians so well, should have known better than that.

The squaw, papoose in her arms, was asleep back in a corner of the room, dark head sunk upon her breast. Mother was knitting a pair of socks for Willie, sitting close to the sputtering candle on the table. I tossed another log into the leaping flames in the fireplace. Snow dropped off it and sizzled and steamed on beds of glowing embers. Willie crept close to my side and waited, all ears, for the story of the big Indian chief.

"Dad," he whispered, "tell him to begin."

"Hush!" I was impatient, too, but knew better than to try to hurry an Indian.

At length Pretty Eagle spoke, words coming slowly as his mind delved far back into the mystery-shrouded past.

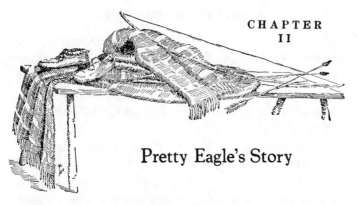

Pretty Eagle's Story

"THE Crows love their land," Pretty Eagle stated, gravely. "That valley of the Echeta Casha* which the White Father in Washington has given them to be theirs as long as there is one Crow left to claim it belonged to them many hundreds of snows ago—before moccasin of white man ever pressed the plains. White Eagle knows I do not speak with crooked tongue?"

I nodded. He went on:

"Nowhere else is to be found such beauty of mountain and valley. There sparkling streams of cold water never dry nor does tall, rich buffalo grass ever wither. The Crows have never feared winter cold nor summer heat for they have had many buffalo and elk to give them food and to clothe them, to shelter them from falling snows and sun's rays. They have had wild geese and ducks and sage hens, deer and antelope. The Great Spirit placed along the streams for His children

*Yellowstone River.

plum thickets, service bushes, chokecherry and bull-berry bushes. The mouths of our papooses are red in spring with strawberries. Everything man needs for his health and happiness is to be found in the valley of the Echeta Casha—the land of the Crows.

"All this White Eagle, friend of the Crow people, already knows. This our enemy, Sioux and Blackfeet and Pawnees, also knew. And, though the Crows said nothing when enemy came to hunt our buffalo, yet the enemy were not satisfied. They wished to possess our beautiful land for their own.

"It is said by our fathers, who were told by their fathers' fathers, that once the Absarokees, known to the palefaces as 'The Crows,' were part of the Gros Ventre tribe, speaking the same language, and that we all came from the Dakotas. We know now only that for many long snows we have lived in this valley extending from the Big Horn Mountains and the Pryors down to the Echeta Casha which the palefaces call the 'Yellowstone River.' "

The big chief, Pretty Eagle, paused and gazed thoughtfully into the fire. He sucked at his empty pipe. I refilled it and lit it and handed it to him. He went on with his story:

"I tell you as my father's father told him and as he told me. Three hundred and fifty snows ago there was a young brave of the Absarokee people named 'Rolling Thunder,' the son of big Chief Sits-

Down-Spotted. This young brave went into a Pawnee camp to take from them picketed horses and make coup. There he saw a Pawnee girl. Her voice was like the soft music of wind in pine trees. Her beauty was the beauty of the sun as it slips down behind the mountains. Her eyes spoke to him and he took her to be his woman and then he forgot the land of his fathers and became a member of the Pawnee tribe. Soon he learned their language and was appointed headman and even became a member of the Pawnee Soldiers' Lodge.

"And when he looked upon his squaw his heart sang, but when he gazed across the valley to the far peaks that sheltered the tepee of Sits-Down-Spotted his heart was heavy.

"Then one day as he, with the members of the Pawnee Soldiers' Lodge, met in council with men of the Shoshones and Sioux and Nez Percés and Blackfeet—men of all tribes except the Absarokees —Rolling Thunder learned that which made his heart cold. They were gathered about the fire— all these wise men—and they talked the sign language, lest even the trees or rocks hear their wicked plans. And he learned that all the tribes meant to band together, after cold had turned the leaves of trees red, and fight the Absarokees, known now as Crows, and take from them their beautiful land.

"When Rolling Thunder learned that, he could not speak. But he knew that more than all else— more than squaw or papoose—he loved his own people and the land that for hundreds of snows had belonged to them. He was married to a Pawnee woman. He had been taken into the Pawnee tribe. They trusted him. But he knew now that he could not fight with them against people of his own blood.

"Silently when the council meeting was over he got up and went away, out into the woods where it was still. He wished to be alone so that he could think what was best for him to do.

"His Pawnee squaw, Breeze-of-the-South-Wind, followed him. 'Where are you going?'

"He looked down at her. She was beautiful and he loved her. He said: 'I am sick. I go to the great warm springs.' (Thermopolis.)

"She gazed into his face. 'I will go with you,' she said, for she knew that he spoke with crooked tongue.

"Rolling Thunder could not meet her eyes. 'No,' he said. 'There are enemy on the warpath. They are scattered like fallen leaves in the wind.'

" 'Yes,' she said. 'I know. And that is why I wish to go with you.'

"He shook his head. 'I am not going to the warm springs. I go to hunt buffalo.'

" 'I can ride,' the Pawnee girl said. 'Not like a squaw, like a brave. Even though we meet many enemies, with you I feel no fear.'

"Then he knew he must speak the truth to his woman. He loved her; they were young; they had known happiness together. 'There is to be war,' he said, 'your people against my people. You are a Pawnee. I am an Absarokee. I go. You stay.'

"She looked at him with flashing eyes. 'Your heart does not speak,' she said, 'only your lips. I am your woman; you are my man.'

"He thought she did not understand. 'I am going back to my father,' he told her, 'and I will fight with him against your people.'

" 'Absarokee—nothing,' she answered, 'Pawnee —nothing. Where you go, I go also.'

"So that night, when all the camp was asleep, Rolling Thunder and his squaw stole away. They rode swift buffalo ponies and led a pack horse loaded with food and clothing, for it was a journey of many sleeps from the Pawnee camp to that of the Absarokee up in the Pryor Mountains. They wound close to the foot of the mountains so they might rush up into cañons and hide if enemy approached, and they traveled the dark trail, resting in the daytime far back among the pines.

"As they rode on, Rolling Thunder and his squaw, his heart was warm with joy. Many snows had passed since he had left his people. Now he was returning to them and with him was the beautiful Pawnee woman. He could not keep the song from his lips but he said to her often during that journey:

" 'You will not grieve for your people?'

"And she would answer him: 'Once, for me,

you gave up your people. Now, for you, I give up my people. I ask only that if there is war you spare my father. He has been kind to you. He is old.'

"And Rolling Thunder promised.

"After many sleeps they came to Pryor Pass which was then, more than three hundred snows ago, just as it is now, a narrow valley with mountains on one side and a high wall of buttes on the other. The blood of the young brave flowed swift and warm in his veins because he was once more in the land of his fathers where every rock and tree and running stream recalled to him adventures of his boyhood.

"But now, as he gazed about, and saw far up the valley, another sleep away, the village of the Absarokees and the big tepee of his father with the golden eagle flashing on its topmost pole, his lips no longer sang. For he knew that the enemy, all the Pawnees and Blackfeet and Cheyennes and Sioux, meant to join and come rushing through that narrow pass and along the valley to attack his people. And he knew that in the valley his people, so few in number, would be slaughtered and their beautiful land lost to them forever.

"He rode on heavy of heart, crossed Pryor Creek, and came to that narrow, high-walled cañon that runs west toward the setting sun. White Eagle remembers the cañon of which I speak?"

"Yes," I told him, "I remember the place."

"Rolling Thunder stopped and looked about

him, back at the pass and the widening valley
through which the enemy would come from the
north, and then at the cañon. He signed for his
squaw to wait and rode a little way up into the
cañon. When he returned she saw that there was
a smile upon his lips."

Pretty Eagle paused to stare into the fire.
Willie's head was heavy against my shoulder and
his wide, eager, unwilling eyes had closed. Gently
I shook him awake. This was history of a time
three hundred years ago and of a race clothed in
mystery—valuable history no white boy could
learn in school books—that the chief was pouring
into white man's ears.

He began speaking again. "We love deeply,"
he said in a lower voice. "Our enemies we hate, but
love for our own sinks down into our hearts and
remains there forever. White Eagle knows?"

"Yes," I said, "I know."

I studied his bronzed face, etched against the
firelight. Rugged and strong and stern, it was,
indeed, the face of a man who could both love and
hate. Time had left marks upon it, lines of suffering, of hardships patiently endured, and of kindliness, but nowhere a hint of meanness nor of
savage cruelty. I deemed it a privilege to be his
friend.

The logs in the fireplace crackled and fell apart,
sending up a flurry of sparks. It was long after
midnight and the storm was over. The wind no

longer whined around the corners of our cabin.
Outside all was a vast white stillness.

I waited without comment until Pretty Eagle
chose to go on with his story.

"There was feasting and dancing in the village
of the Absarokees that night, for the son of their
chief had returned. A crier rode through the village chanting strange words until all the people
came running out from tepees to hear his message.
And he cried:

" 'Rolling Thunder has returned and has
brought with him the Pawnee woman, Breeze-of-
the-South-Wind, daughter of Chief Red Tomahawk.'

"Then all the Mountain Crows and all the River
Crows put on their feast costumes and gathered
around the campfire and there was feasting and
dancing and singing and speech-making.

"But when the feasting was over and squaws
and children had gone to their tepees, when there
remained around the fire only chiefs and headmen
and medicine men, runners and wolves, then Rolling Thunder spoke.

" 'My heart sings,' he told them, 'because I am
once more with my own people.'

"Then the father, Chief Sits-Down-Spotted,
drew a few puffs from his red stone pipe and
touched the bowl to the ground. He held it aloft
and gazed at it in silence. Then he pointed the
stem to the east, the west, the north, the south.
White Eagle knows our customs."

"Yes," I nodded, "I know."

"After the peace-pipe smoke Rolling Thunder rose and spoke: 'I have come from the land of the Pawnees, the land of our enemy. The enemy are as many as the blades of grass on our plains. They know that though we, the Absarokees, are brave of heart, we are few. They desire our land with its many fat buffaloes and deer and mountain sheep, its tall grasses and running streams. Before another moon they will come down from the north, through the pass into our valley, Pawnees and Cheyennes and Sioux and Blackfeet, to take from us our horses and our land, to slaughter our squaws and papooses. They have already started on the warpath and have come as far as Clarks Fork and the mouth of Wind River. There they have camps. From these camps they send signals and, at the proper moment, they will join and rush in upon us. We cannot escape. There are mountains where the sun rises and mountains where the sun sets. They will trap us in our valley like bear in a cave. I have spoken.'

"Rolling Thunder sat down.

"His father, Sits-Down-Spotted, asked him: 'All this you know? You speak not idle squaw talk?'

" 'All this I know,' Rolling Thunder said. 'I have heard members of the Soldiers' Lodge make plans. My woman, Breeze-of-the-South-Wind, heard Pawnee wolves talk after they had been on lookout peaks where they could see all the valley of the Absarokees. Before another moon they will be upon us.' "

Willie, wide awake now, burst out impatiently: "But they didn't get licked, did they? You Crows won, didn't you?"

Chief Pretty Eagle smiled at my son. "All this," he reminded us, "happened three hundred snows ago. The Crows still live in their valley of the Echeta Casha. I tell you the story as my father's father told it to him.

"In the valley south of Pryor Pass, near Pryor Creek, even today, are mounds covered with stones and overgrown with greasewood, two very high mounds and many smaller ones. Some say they are to mark an old trail, but that is not so. No paleface knows their history. All Indians riding by, even to this day, add a stone to the pile, though few understand why. They do not know they are erecting a monument to Crow warriors killed in the fiercest battle ever fought by Indian tribes."

Pretty Eagle had quite forgotten his audience and was merely voicing old memories as he gazed soberly into our fire, transporting us back against the current of years.

"It was the time when wild geese fly south to winter sun. Runners were sent to warn River Crows and soon they came to join the Mountain Crows, bringing with them squaws and papooses, horses and dogs. And yet, though all the valley

between mountain ranges was covered with tepees
of our people, we were to our enemy as but one
star in the Blue. Wolves stationed on high points
looking across rivers and cañons and valleys
watched for approach of the foe, while swift runners waited their signals, ready to dash into camp
with messages.

"In Crow village everyone was busy, hearts
heavy with anxiety. For, if our enemy won in the
terrible battle soon to take place, then those of our
people who were left would be driven from their
land of plenty and must take with them all they
could carry of food and clothing. So the squaws
worked from rising sun to its setting, worked for
their men and children and the country they loved.
They cut up the meat the hunters were bringing
in daily from the kill and hung it up to dry. They
gathered bull-berries for pemmican—enough to
fill all their parfleche boxes. They made moccasins
and bed robes and body robes and covers of buffalo
hides for the tepees.

"Meanwhile some of the men hunted buffalo
and others made war clubs and strong bows and
many sharp arrows. And each night, when Old
Woman was high in the Blue, all the wise men
gathered around the council fire and talked war
talk. And some thought they should do this and
some thought they should do that. But Rolling
Thunder said:

" 'We dare not fight our enemy in the open
for we are too few.'

"The eyes of Chief Sits-Down-Spotted flashed. 'Would you have us run from the enemy as buffalo runs from the hunter?'

"Rolling Thunder sprang to his feet. 'I have a plan! As I, with my Pawnee woman, came from the south through Pryor Pass I saw a cañon, narrow and high, running west from the valley. I would have all our warriors, save fifty young men, gather in that cañon with food for many days and war clubs and arrows. I would have our squaws fix bushes and small trees across the opening as though they grew there. Then, when our wolves tell us the enemy is approaching from Wind River and Clark Fork, I would lead fifty young braves close to the Pass through which they must come. We would be mounted on the swiftest of buffalo ponies. We would seem to the enemy not warriors, only young men hunting. They would pursue us and we would lead them on, though beyond reach of their arrows, until they had shot them all toward us. Then, when all their arrows were used, we would dash past the mouth of the cañon and the Crow warriors hidden there could spring out upon them. If our medicine is strong and if the Great Spirit is kind to us we shall save our land for our children and our children's children forever. I have spoken.'

"Old Chief Sits-Down-Spotted said nothing, but his heart sang for it was his son who had spoken wise words.

"One of the warriors said: 'The heart of Rolling Thunder is young but his head is old. We will do in all things as he advises.'

" 'Then,' said Rolling Thunder, 'let us waken squaws and papooses and move camp at once, traveling the dark trail, so enemy wolves cannot see and guess our plans.'

"As the young brave had said, so it was done. Before another sleep all our Crow people, except fifty young men, were concealed back in the cañon along Pryor Creek with horses and dogs and food to last many sleeps. And while they waited behind the blind of pine trees that our squaws had thrust into the ground, many times the Old Woman rose high in the Blue and sank behind mountain peaks. And still our wolves on lookout points saw no sign of approaching enemy.

"But, after many sleeps, one morning early the Crows heard a dull rumbling they knew to be the beat of thousands of hoofs upon the earth. Soon large herds of buffalo came pouring through the pass and into the valley as though they were being driven. Soon all the valley was dark with them.

"Squaws said: 'The Great Spirit is kind to his children, the Crows. He loves us best. He is sending all the buffalo in the world to us.'

"But Rolling Thunder said: 'The time has come. Our enemy must be advancing in such vast numbers that they cover all the valley of Echeta Casha Asha, driving buffaloes ahead of them. Now I, with my fifty braves, will hurry to the Pass and pretend to hunt buffaloes and lead the enemy to the cañon.'

"He was about to leap upon his horse, but the Pawnee woman, Breeze-of-the-South-Wind, ran up to him and stood before him, her hand upon his arm.

" 'You are going to fight my people,' she said. 'It is well, for I am your woman and my heart is with your people, the Absarokees. But my father, Red Tomahawk, Chief of the Pawnees, is old. His heart beats slow, his sinews are tired. He desired peace with your people but when his young men talked big war talk he could do nothing. If you win in today's battle I ask that you spare my father.'

"Rolling Thunder looked down into the face of his woman, looked long, for he might never see her again. His heart was heavy. He said: 'If I live I will bring your father safe back to you.'

" 'And if an enemy's arrow pierces your heart, then another shall pierce mine and I will join you in the Happy Hunting Ground, for I would not wish to remain long upon earth without you.'

"Then Rolling Thunder and his fifty braves rode slowly on southward toward Pryor Pass, shooting at buffalo, a song upon their lips. They followed the trail past the high peak of red stone which stands there today, just as it did three hundred snows ago. And things happened as they had planned. The enemy came pouring through Pryor

Pass like waters of a great river, all the tribes of the south, joined against the Absarokees. They came yelling their war cries and waving their tomahawks. They wore war bonnets that trailed on the ground. Their faces were ugly with paint.

"And when they saw the little band of young Crow hunters running from them like rabbits making for their holes, they rent the air with war whoops. They quirted their horses and filled the air with arrows that fell harmlessly just back of the fleeing Crows. And the Crows scurried this way and that across the valley, trying to dodge arrows, trying to lead the enemy on toward the cañon.

"You palefaces know that valley. Your cattle graze there. You go to build camp fires on Pryor Creek and make coffee and then lie down to sleep where all is peace and stillness, without thought of fear. None of you know of that day three hundred and fifty years ago when hearts beat fast with fear, when the air was loud with shrieks of warriors, when the long grass was stained red with blood of Crow and Sioux and Pawnee and Cheyenne, when the pure waters of the creek were dammed by heaped-up bodies of the dying, staggering there, mad with thirst.

"You speak of the beautiful valley as 'The Crow Reservation,' given us by the White Father. You do not know that the Crows bought that land with their lives, paid for it in suffering and blood.

"Some few of Rolling Thunder's braves fell

that day under shower of enemy arrows. When he thought that most of the arrows had been spent, he, with those of his men who were left, dashed back across Pryor Creek and past the mouth of the cañon. On he went with his small band, the enemy close at heel, yelling, ready to spring on them with war clubs and scalping knives, riding into the trap set for them.

"Suddenly the thick forest of little trees fell as though before a strong wind and from out the cañon, closing in upon the surprised enemy, poured all the hidden Crow warriors. They were still out-numbered three to one, but their horses were fresh and their arrows many and they were fighting for that which was nearest their hearts—home and children.

"All through the long day they fought until the air was filled with the whine of flying arrows and shrieks of wounded horses and moans of dying men. Men pulled arrows out of dead bodies to use them over again. They fought hand-to-hand with war clubs and knives. They fought until, as the sun sank down behind the mountains, those of the enemy who were spared went crawling back through the Pass to their camps on Wind River, leaving dead and dying.

"Then the victorious Crows killed dying war-riors and dying horses, to end their suffering. And they placed bodies in piles—both the enemy and their own people—one at the foot of Red Rock

Peak, another farther north along the trail and
still others as they fell, here and there across the
valley. They placed beside them strips of dried
meat to last them on the journey across the Slippery Log, and war clubs, and the bodies of their
horses. Then they covered all with mounds of
earth and stones. That was over three hundred
years ago but the mounds are still there. White
Eagle has seen them."

"Yes," I said, "I have seen those mounds."

"I, Pretty Eagle, Chief of the Mountain Crows,
have told this to my white brother, White Eagle.
It is the story of the fiercest battle ever fought between Indian tribes. He will put it into a book for
palefaces to read so they may understand why the
Absarokees whom you speak of as 'Crows' love
their land, the valley of the Echeta Casha Asha,
with such a deep love. It was purchased with the
blood of brave men. I have spoken."

It was almost morning. The logs were burned
low and the room was chill. It was with difficulty
I brought myself back to the present, so vividly had
I shared with Pretty Eagle that harrowing time of
long ago. I kicked the embers into flame and added
another log.

Pretty Eagle sat silent. There was a smile on his
strong, bronzed, wrinkled face as he lost himself
in the glory of a day that was gone.

"But say!" Willie piped up, "what became of
Red Tomahawk?"

The big chief sighed and smiled. "Rolling Thunder captured him early in the battle and hid him safely in the cañon back of the trees. That night he was led to the camp of the Crows and there, with his daughter and Rolling Thunder, he lived out his days in peace and happiness."

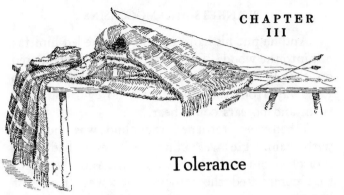

Tolerance

ALMOST daily there is to be seen on Hardin streets a blind Indian man, led along by one child or another. He is twenty-five years old. He walks slowly, staring straight ahead, head held high. He appears to be tranquil, even happy. There is no shadow of bitterness on his face.

It is said that twenty years ago, as he was approaching school age, he was told that he must attend the white man's school. He wept, he sulked, he rebelled. Like most Crow Indians he was both fiercely proud and painfully shy and he shrank from mingling with white boys who, he knew, would ridicule his dress and manners and dark skin. For days the child was like a wild thing at bay and his young heart beat fast with fear. He clung sobbing to his father and mother, but, though they too were frightened, and would have kept him with them, they were powerless against the mandates of the white man.

Then the old grandmother said to the little boy, "Come with me."

And he put his hand in hers and she led him far out into the woods. For a long while they wandered on, the old woman and the boy, until they were so far away from the village that no eyes could see them and no ears could hear.

When they returned the child was moaning with pain. He was blind. His eyes had been scratched out with a sharp stick. And the hands that committed the atrocious act were hands of love.

"Now," the old woman explained, calmly, tenderly, "our little boy will not have to go to the school of the white man."

Apparently, for reasons which we should try to understand, that civilization which seems so right and proper to us and which we have endeavored so zealously to force upon our wards is no more admirable to them than is theirs to us.

If it were given us to see into the terrorized heart of that old ignorant Indian woman who chose to blind for life the little boy she loved rather than commit him to the mercies of the conquerors of her race we might approach toward an understanding of why the Indian has been disinclined to respond to the cultural atmosphere with which we have surrounded him.

Two Indian women, one day during the Midland Empire Fair, were playing "Housie." One of them was very pretty; both, because of their youth and high spirits, were attractive. They wore new calico dresses and high-topped beaded moccasins. Over their heads, framing olive-tinted animated faces, were gaudy silk handkerchiefs, folded cross-wise. They talked gayly in very good English as they arranged beans on called-out numbers and occasionally flashed bright-eyed friendly glances toward their palefaced competitors.

They were young, it was fair-time, they were all dressed up in their very best clothes, and the intoxication of folks in uproarious holiday mood was upon them. They were obviously having a very good time, glad to be a joyous part of the hilarious crowd.

Presently one of them held up a slim hand and called out: "Housie!" She had won a pound of coffee. Her dark eyes sparkled. Quickly, from a knotted handkerchief, she extracted a dime, ready to try her luck again.

But a man standing near her, a white man belonging to the race that prides itself upon its civilization and superior culture, glanced up, scowling, from his housie board and burst out in an irascible voice loud enough for all to hear: "I wish you'd take that dirty brat of yours and get out of here!"

There was, it is true, a small Indian lad standing near, and his face was dirty. He had an ice cream cone in one hand and a caramelized apple in the other. He was endeavoring, with more or less success, to eat both at the same time, and his earnest efforts were leaving their mark upon his

chubby countenance. But that he did not belong
to either of the college-bred young Indian women
the irate white gentleman never paused to consider. He paused to consider nothing save the in-
disputable fact that he belonged to the ruling race
and that the presence of those savages annoyed
him.

His snarl had its effect. Instantly the smiles
froze on the fine, intelligent dark faces. For a
second they stood, stunned by the brutal insult,
flushing under the glances focused upon them.
Their eyes flashed anger. They were deeply hurt
down to the very soul of them. Without a word,
joy quite dispelled, they left the game and walked
slowly away.

Doubtless no one could convince those Indian
girls that the man whose remark cut deep into their
hearts, oversensitive to ridicule, does not epito-
mize the entire cultured white race. He was well
dressed. He had smooth, white hands, and, until
he spoke, gave no indication that he was not a
gentleman. In their minds he stood, and will
always stand, as representative of the race that dubs
them "savages." For they have the same inclina-
tion to generalize concerning the whites as the
whites have concerning them.

They knew that the irritable gentleman, regardless of how much he were annoyed, would
never have presumed to so insult a white woman
in public. That he dared do so to them, and with

an air testifying that he considered himself quite within his rights, there was only one reason: they were Indians.

Unfortunately the attitude of too many whites toward the Indians is one of settled prejudice, amounting to antagonism. It strengthens the barrier between the two races, that antagonism, and prohibits any thorough understanding of a people naturally fine, kindly, intelligent, talented, and unhappy.

The shame is ours, and the loss, that by an inexcusably gross handling of a delicate situation we have forfeited the inestimable privilege of seeing into the heart of the Indian, for there is rare beauty and courage hidden deep within. Even we, their conquerors, if we chose, might at this late day win their confidence and friendship, since they are charitable and perhaps a little lonely and frightened, so few of them are left. Instead, having possessed their land, prohibited their free, glad, wild life, and then, in recompense, doled out to them so many acres of land, so many yards of calico, so many pounds of meat, we regard them with the amused interest we vouchsafe an animal in the zoo.

Or those zealous ones among us who have the reformer's itch work ourselves—and them—into a frenzy, endeavoring to prove to them that our way is the only right way and our God the only God.

Meanwhile the bewildered victims of so many bungling experiments, having learned by lessons many and bitter that might makes right, wrap their blankets about them and hold themselves aloof from the civilization that goes rushing, buzzing, whizzing, clanging past their ears.

In an Indian village it is an unheard-of thing for one to lock his door against another. Nor is any man allowed to suffer hunger while his neighbor has enough for two. But they hear of how their white brother dares not go to bed at night without locking his door against some thieving paleface; and of how, in cities, palefaces are shot down without warning by other palefaces as they walk along the streets; and of how many of them dare not venture out, except in armoured cars; and of how there are long lines of hungry men, waiting in patient formation for a bite of bread, because a very few palefaces have managed to corner all the wealth of the land. And they recall, these savages whom we are endeavoring to civilize, that only a few years ago their plains were rich in all a man could need for health and happiness, and that there was an abundance for all, without nerve-racking toil or theft or murder.

The Indian knows that back of civilization's complicated system of commerce, its monetary exchanges, its inventions, its buzzing wheels within wheels, its shrieking factory whistles and chug of motors, its soul-devastating scramble to accumu-

late money and ever more money, he knows that
back of all that lies the simple, elementary need of
man for food and clothing and shelter and leisure
in which to enjoy life. And he goes his way and
ponders and smiles because his white brother pre-
sumes to declare that the way of the whites is best,
that the Indian is savage and the paleface civilized.

To the savage, civilized whites are a riddle.
Why? Why? Why a heap-big house with many
idle rooms to furnish and clean when the curtain-
partitioned tepee has for countless snows sufficed?
Why back-breaking toil up and down narrow
strips of land, pushing a plow, in order to raise feed
for pigs and cows so that they may be killed and
eaten when formerly vast unfenced plains were
freckled thick with buffalo grazing on tall, thick,
luxuriant grass?

It seems to the Indian that his white brother,
having ruthlessly destroyed all the generous gifts
of the Great Spirit, is now slaving feverishly to
recover them. Verily, the ways of the paleface,
though undoubtedly the right and only ways, are
past finding out.

Not all Indians, however, are averse to modern
methods of livelihood. In an agricultural assembly
a few weeks ago a middle-aged, dignified Indian
who as president of one of the chapters occupied a
conspicuous seat in the front row, stood up to
make a speech.

"We like farming," he said, impressively, in his

best oratorical style. "We like pigs. Cows. But most of all we like poultry. We like poultry pretty much. Poultry lay eggs. Eggs make cake. Cake heap good. Indians like cake pretty much."

The mind of the Crow Indian is alert, inquisitive, often intellectual. Among them are thinkers, philosophers, musicians, artists, orators. Knowing that they have gifts for the world, yet they hug those gifts to themselves, because they believe the world has no use for them.

And perplexities continue to baffle them. Why schools? they ask. And that, to the red man, is the most pregnant and tragic query of all.

This is how, with cutting sarcasm, Hamlin Garland, in his book, *The American Indian,* answers that query: "You are all fools. Your religion is wicked and you are not fit to teach your children. My religion—my God—is the only God that is true and righteous and I will take your children in order that you may be taught the true path and become as the white man."

The Indian school at Crow has been closed because politicians deem it an unnecessary extravagance, and the Indian children must attend the public school at Hardin. There they rub shoulder to shoulder, soul to soul, with white children, enduring snobbery and arrogance. They know they are not wanted—those little, frightened, intensely proud Indian boys and girls. Their clothes are ridiculed, and their speech, and their dark skins. In a thousand subtle ways they are tortured as only young human animals know how to torture.

Major Pratt, sensing the crying need of the Indians for a school of their own where they could be removed from the grueling superiority of white children, founded Carlisle College. That school has sent out many fine Indian women and men, citizens of whom any nation might well be proud. But politicians decided that Carlisle was an unnecessary extravagance, so, in 1917 it was closed and is now being used by the army for medical training.

Fortunately such conditions do not exist everywhere. On the Blackfeet Reserve Indian children attend public schools, but it so happens that there they outnumber white children ten to one. Consequently, escaping the humiliating pricks of racial antagonism, they are making long strides toward a cultural life. They have a glee club and debating society, an orchestra and a band. Many of them are outstanding members of the 4-H Club. They are proving to a doubting world what Indian children, given a chance, may become.

And still the question repeats itself—why schools? Indians know that often a higher education serves only as a perpetual, refined torment for them. Seldom, in the white man's world, is the Indian who would make his living by brain power given a fighting chance in competition with the white man. It is a current belief that education is wasted on an Indian, because, after twelve or sixteen years of grade and high school, and possibly college, he reverts to type, drifts back to blanket and moccasin and tepee. Too often this is true, but those who have taken pains to spread the propaganda have failed to explain why it is so.

In addition to the competition all youth faces, young Indians starting out in life must contend against racial competition as well.

An Indian lad graduates from law school. To his very fingertips he is alive with courage, hope, fine enthusiasm, eager to prove that he is a "koe-nig," a "kan-ning," a "man who knows and can." In his veins flows the blood of countless generations of men who endured gruelling torments to test their physical and mental capacity for suffering so they might prove themselves worthy of chieftain-ship. He, like those distinctive men of his race, is ambitious for the glory of achievement. And he knows, as did his classmates in college, that the Great Spirit has blessed—or cursed—him with a shrewd mind, clear-thinking, far-seeing, analytical.

And so, spurred on by the blind optimism of youth, he rents and furnishes an office. And there he waits for clients who do not come, waits hope-fully, patiently, grimly. He listens to footsteps coming down the corridor, but they never pause at his door, they go on to the adjoining office where a classmate of his, a white boy, has begun the prac-tice of law.

And the Indian lad asks, "Why? Why?"

But he knows the answer. It is because he, who must live in a white man's country, is an Indian and has been cursed with a copper skin.

Heartsick, homesick, penniless, he at last gives up, goes out the door of his office, closing it upon dead hopes, and returns to his people. And his old mother says to him: "You know now that I did not speak with crooked tongue when I told you there is no place in the white man's world for the Indian."

Yes, he knows now. He has become a misfit everywhere. The simple life of his people no longer satisfies him. His brief sojourn in the white man's world has left him bruised and shocked. As he trudges behind the plow he thinks bitter thoughts. In the olden days there would have been outlet for youth's surcharged energy in mad dashes across the plains after buffalo, in facing danger, taking enemies' picketed horses, defending his own against theft. But now, while his hand guides the plow, his mind thinks and broods.

Chief Plenty Coups, wise, tender, saddened old man, comprehends all the problems his young men must meet and must somehow solve in this, for them, difficult period of readjustment. Sorrowfully he admits that few of the boys returning from college go up onto the mountain top to await visions. Instead, many of them seek momentary happiness in whiskey or in "that other very bad weed that is shipped in and that makes the boys see visions—but not good visions."

He knows they are not bad, only bewildered and bitter and disillusioned. He knows that impetuous, high-spirited, hot-headed youth cannot be expected at once to accept with patient resignation a situation that galls and humiliates.

Indians! The very word had power to send chills of fear up the spine of the school boy as he bent over his history book and read about the savage red man and his war upon the white settlers. The Indian set fire to the homes of the settlers and danced about them while they burned. He set the forests to ringing with his hideous war whoop. He scalped people. He was cruel, bloodthirsty, treacherous.

But historians often failed to make it plain to the shivering school boy that the Indians were from the first fighting a defensive war, fighting to hold against invaders the land they loved, the land that had been theirs for hundreds of years.

Nor did historians state that the savage whom they painted with war bonnet and blood-dripping tomahawk was a kind father, loving his children with a deep, protective, very beautiful love. Nor that he was warring at great odds, against vastly superior numbers, to guard his home and the lives of his children. Cruel? Treacherous? Not more so than the palefaces who were fencing his hunting grounds and destroying his only means of livelihood. War always, between all races, is cruelty, treachery.

Mary, daughter of Chief Pretty Eagle. She said to Dr. Allen: "I give this picture to our friend, White Eagle, because, when I was a little girl, he saved the lives of my father, my mother, and myself." Photograph by Goff.

The Crow Indian is not by nature cruel. He is kind and tender to children and to animals. In the Crow village are many dogs. They are well-fed happy mongrels, ready to greet you with a gay tail-wag. Never have I seen one slink or cower as though accustomed to abuse. Dr. Allen says that in the three years he served on the Crow Reservation as government blacksmith he did not see an Indian strike a dog or abuse a horse.

During the week of the Midland Empire Fair the Crow tribe are welcome guests of the Fair Board. An attractive strip of ground beside the river bank is placed at their disposal, and there they set up tepees, cook over open fires, suffer good-naturedly the gaze of the curious, and enter gayly into the festive spirit of the occasion. They like to dress in their very best clothes and wander about carnival grounds. One sees them everywhere lending picturesque color: family groups, father and mother with small, excited children clamoring for pop and merry-go-round rides; pretty girls in gay blankets sauntering along, eyes bright and shy, arms encircling one another's waists; young men smoking cigarettes, intensely interested in the races, yet always obviously aware of the bright-eyed girls. Clean, quiet, well-mannered people, all of them, holding themselves aloof from the whites with a natural dignity that has in it nothing of arrogance nor of servility.

It is a revelation to watch them, their enthusiasm, their indulgence to their children.

A tall grave-faced Crow, wearing cheap "store" trousers, bright flannel shirt and moccasins, his thin braids of black hair framing a dark, rugged face, was being led along by his two small sons who, with fixed singleness of purpose, were tugging at his hands.

"Hey!" one of them shouted, "you promised to give us a ride on the merry-go-round!"

At once the man purchased tickets and placed the two lads on horses. He paused to fasten a little shirt that had come unbuttoned. As he performed that simple, fatherly task his face wore a patient tenderness, a benignancy, that was most beautiful. Quite unaware of observation, absorbed in the happiness of his children, the man revealed at that moment a glimpse of a soul that must also be beautiful.

During fair-week we had the pleasure of visiting Simon Bull-tail and his wife in their tepee. They received us with courteous hospitality. Mrs. Bull-tail had just taken down her hair and was combing it. It was parted in the middle and hung on either side of her face in soft waves, not black, though she is a full-blood Crow, but dark brown with warm glints in it. Her face, undoubtedly beautiful in youth, was still attractive, a face of character, pleasant, with fineness and strength. Across the room three small daughters were playing.

Doctor Allen asked Mrs. Bull-tail, "Do you remember Chief Pretty Eagle?"

"Oh, yes," she said at once. "I was about eight years old when he died, but I remember him."

"Do you know anything about his daughter Mary?"

"Why, yes. Now, let me see. He had three daughters. One died. One married Yellow-tail and one—now wait, it's a long while ago—let me get it straight—I think Mary is now Mrs. Stewart. She lives on the Crow Reservation."

"Pretty Eagle and I," Doctor Allen said, "were friends long ago."

She smiled. "Oh, yes," she said. "I've heard about that. You are White Eagle. You saved their lives once when they were lost in a blizzard, Pretty Eagle and his squaw, and his girl, Mary."

Just then there was an uproar on the other side of the tent. One of the daughters, the smallest, was crying loudly.

"What's the matter?" I asked in alarm. Having been told so often that Indian children never laugh, never cry, I judged the present outburst of grief must have been prompted by something very serious.

Ignoring my question our host made some remark concerning Chief Plenty Coups, whom we were expecting any moment.

The little girl continued to weep.

"What *is* the matter?" I demanded.

The father and mother, calmly deaf to the sobs of their naughty child, were endeavoring to carry on the conversation with their guests. But finally my insistence won its reward.

"I think," Simon Bull-tail told me, smiling, "her sister put a finger in her eye."

Suddenly as the storm had burst peace was restored. The children began laughing.

And then, over our heads, the glance of husband and wife met, and I caught there a flash of patient indulgence, of paternal pride shared, of comradeship that was charming.

"What will you do with your naughty little daughter?" I inquired. "Will you whip her?"

And then the Indian, Simon Bull-tail, born of a race known for their atrocious cruelty, looked straight into my eyes. In his own was puzzled pity, possibly contempt.

"Indians," he informed me, cuttingly, "do not wheep their children."

Crow Indians do not believe in corporal punishment. Punishment of any kind, we gathered, has never been a vital consideration either with the family or the tribe.

"Supposing one of your tribe commits a crime, steals, or kills another, what would happen to him?"

After a moment's thought Simon Bull-tail answered brightly, like a school boy sure of his lesson, "The electric chair."

"Yes, but before you were under white man's laws what would have been done to punish him?"

"The chief would have had him wheeped and sent away. No one of us would have spoken to him."

To the Crow Indian, with his proud spirit, peculiarly sensitive to ridicule, no conceivable punishment would have been less endurable than public shame and banishment from the social life of his people.

In the early day of the Colonists we know that Chief Massasoit cordially welcomed the Pilgrims to his shores. When he died his son, Wamsutta, became chief. He, too, befriended the whites and trusted them. Yet the invading palefaces, led by Winslow, convinced that all Indians were savages and dangerous, attacked the young chief in his lodge. Never dreaming of enmity, Wamsutta was unarmed and had with him only eighty of his braves. Winslow, pistol pointed, took him captive and led him bound to the fort. The young chief, proud, utterly astonished, was naturally indignant and deeply hurt, so much so that he became ill and was allowed to return to his home.

Elliott concludes the episode: "He died on his way. He was carried home on the shoulders of his men and borne silently to his silent grave near Mount Hope, in the evening of the day, and in the prime of his life, between lines of sad, quick-minded men, who well believed him the victim of injustice and ingratitude; for his father had been the ally of England and so was he, and the like in-

dignity had not before been put upon any
sachem."

Yet the school boy bending over his history
book, reading, while shivers go up and down his
spine, of the horrors of "King Philip's War," does
not always understand that that war was incited
by a devoted brother's thirst for revenge. Philip
had loved his brother. He knew that Wamsutta
could never find rest for his spirit in the Happy
Hunting Ground until his death had been avenged.

Still, even then, so insists Patton in his *History
of the American People,* "The colonists could now
have warded off strife by conciliating the Indians.
No effort was made to soothe their wounded feel-
ings; they were treated as bloody heathen whom it
was their duty, as 'the chosen of the Lord,' to drive
out of the land."

And at the close of the war, when the odds
were so overwhelmingly against the Indians,
Philip's spirit was crushed. He exclaimed, "My
heart breaks. I am ready to die."

Patton goes on: "After Philip's death his
orphan boy was to be disposed of. The last prince
of the Wampanoags, the grandson of the generous
old Massasoit who had welcomed the Pilgrims and
had given them his friendship, was sent to toil as
a slave under the burning sun of Bermuda."

And after that, with a gross insolence that
would be laughable were it not so tragic, the
whites sent missionaries to "convert" the Indians,

to teach them that the white man's God is a tender and loving Father.

An attitude of intolerance or patronizing arrogance toward a suppressed and helpless people does not promise for its rulers a great and happy future. A race with its foot on the neck of its subjects cannot hope long to stand upright.

Theodore Roosevelt has written: "We Americans can do our allotted task well only if we face it steadily and bravely, seeing but not fearing the dangers. Above all we must stand shoulder to shoulder, not asking as to ancestry or creed of our comrades, but only demanding that they be in very truth Americans, and that we work together, heart, hand, and head, for the honor and the greatness of our common country."

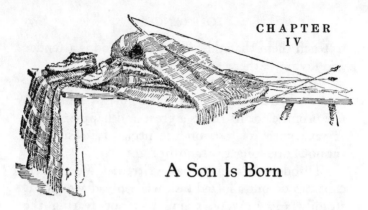

A Son Is Born

MANY snows ago, in a tepee in the land of buffalo, the land of mountains and running water, the land of the Absarokees, there was born a black-eyed, dark-skinned baby boy. And the heart of the dark-skinned young mother sang. She held him close in her arms and cuddled him and crooned over him quite like mothers the world over. And, like all mothers, she thought her baby the strongest and prettiest and best baby, the most wonderful baby, that ever reached up tiny arms to the Blue.

Tenderly and wisely she cared for him, her mind always upon him, even while she attended to the manifold duties of the young Indian wife. To make sure that his limbs grew straight as a sapling shoot she took a board and padded it with buffalo robes until it was a soft nest and bound him to it. She fastened a bent willow in an arch over the board so that, if ever the cradle fell, her baby's face would be protected. And to that arch, within reach of small groping hands, she tied playthings that she had fashioned during the months of waiting: a cluster of small rib-bones, highly polished, brightly painted, that rattled in the breeze; a bit of quaking asp wood carved into the shape of a tomahawk; a beaded elk-hide bag filled with pebbles that tinkled pleasantly.

Whenever she went out into the woods to gather berries for pemmican, bull, juniper, or hawthorne, or out onto the plains to cut up the meat of the buffalo which her men hunters had killed, she strapped the cradle on her back and carried her baby with her. Often while she worked she tied the cradle to the limb of a tree and the breeze rocked it gently and the baby, warm and comfortable in his cozy nest, gazed up into the thick branches and laughed and crowed until he fell asleep. But she paused in her work at once, if he even so much as whimpered, to take him in her arms and soothe him, for she loved him, and she believed that only wicked mothers suffer their children to cry.

So, for many moons, he let it be known when he was hungry, and kicked and laughed lustily when his stomach was full, as do little human animals everywhere. As he grew older, stronger, he began creeping about, exploring that small world of his confined by the buffalo-hide walls of the tepee. Later, with his mother's loving hand guarding against too near an approach to the fire, he ventured wavering steps. By the time snows were gone and grass in the low places had begun to show green his legs were so sturdy that he was permitted to toddle out with his older brother close to his mother's tepee. And his bright, dark, unspeculative eyes took in the immensity of a land roofed by the sky and walled by the purple mist-tinted mountains, that land which had, for a time longer than the oldest man of the tribe could remember, belonged to the Absarokee people, known to the palefaces as the "Crows."

And so, before he could speak in terms of beauty, almost before he could speak at all, the soul of the boy A-Leek-Chea-Ahoosh, destined to fame as Plenty Coups, chief of all the tribes of the Northwest, became saturated with the beauty of the land of his fathers. That beauty was a vital part of him as he was an inseparable part of the land he loved.

To make his body strong his mother plunged him daily into the icy waters of Mission Creek. To instill courage into the young heart she sent him out alone at night into the whispering darkness of the forest to gather wood for her fire. And often, he says, when he came panting back to the tepee, eyes wide with fright of all the queer rustling noises of the dark, she took the wood from him and tossed it on the fire and bade him go after more. "Because," she told him, sternly, "a brave boy would not have run. A brave boy would have walked slowly through the dark, fearing nothing."

Sometimes, being high-spirited and strong-willed, he was naughty. One particular time he stole all the sweet cakes his mother had been keeping for a feast day. His mother, of course, did not whip him, for Indians do not believe in whipping children. She devised a far more cruel punishment —she ridiculed him and ostracized him, for all of one long day, from the family social life. And she made him understand that brave men, when one trusts to their honor, do not steal. But she sang him to sleep, nights, with songs that had to do with courageous warriors who crept into enemies' camps and took their picketed horses. For that was not theft; that was war.

Although the father of A-Leek-Chea-Ahoosh died when the boy was still too young to remember him, he suffered no lack of fatherly care, for his uncle, the brother of his father, was kind to him. He was a skillful hunter, that uncle, and the family tepee was always filled with dried elk meat and pemmican and "boss" ribs and fat buffalo tongues. But it was the mother, wise, stern, conscientious, loving, who prepared her son for the part he was to play in life.

The little Indian boy, A-Leek-Chea-Ahoosh, together with his older brother, spent a happy childhood, brimful of escapades. The uncle made them skiis and the two went wallowing out through the snow to slide down the steep mountain side. He made them a sled from a hollow log and the boys dragged it, heavily loaded, across bare ground until its bottom was very smooth. Then they dragged it up on the mountain and sat in it, the older brother in front, A-Leek-Chea-Ahoosh behind, and went skimming down, down, and far across the white plain, so fast that the wind sang to them.

They skated on the creek when it was frozen. Often they played with other children from neighboring tepees and built forts of snow. Then they divided into two sides, the one group the brave Crows, the other, their cruel enemy, the Blackfeet. And always the older brother was chief of the Crows and chose A-Leek-Chea-Ahoosh to be his best warrior or runner or "wolf," and the two sides scouted around for safer ambush and hurled snowballs. And always the Crow side won against the enemy and pretended to scalp them and take their picketed horses.

Plenty Coups remembers summer nights while he was still a small boy, lying on the ground close to his mother's side, and feeling the warmth of the big camp fire creep over his body, and watching the flames go leaping and crackling up into the blackness of the forest. He stared up through the trees to where the Old Woman sailed swiftly across the Blue. And he tried very hard to keep awake and listen to the tales the men were telling, his uncle and the other warriors, of their attacks on the enemy, but the pines sang to him, and the waters of the creek, and lulled him to sleep.

Years later, after A-Leek-Chea-Ahoosh had made so many coups that he became known as "Plenty Coups," he and his paleface brother Allen spent much time out on the plains hunting buffalo. Then, weary after a hard day, the two young men would lie close to their camp fire and Plenty Coups would relate to his friend "White Eagle" stories of his boyhood.

"I will tell to White Eagle," he would say, as he lay smoking, gazing up into the night sky, "the story of my childhood. I will tell him of my life when I was so high." And he extended his hand, measuring the height of a lad of six. "And I will tell him of my life when I was so high." And he raised his hand. "The rest," he added, "White Eagle knows.

"I can recall," Plenty Coups said, "long winter nights after the sun had slipped back of the mountains when all was warm and cozy in my mother's tepee. Then we gathered close to the fire, my mother, my uncle, my brother, my dog, and myself, often with visitors from neighboring tepees. We could hear the falling snow sifting through the dry branches of the trees outside, and the howl of a wolf from far across the still white plains, and the shriek of the East Wind. Always my mother, sitting a little apart from the men, bent over the work she loved, beading beautiful moccasins for my brother or me, or polishing the carved handles of tomahawks which we would carry in dances

when we were bigger. While she worked, fashion-
ing from beads flowers like those that grow on
the plains, she sometimes sang to us the songs of
the bravery of our people. Sometimes our uncle
would relate tales of long past wars and of how the
Crows had taken many scalps and captured many
enemy horses, and of how they had always held
their beautiful land against all enemy tribes, until
they had become known as the bravest and richest
people in the world.

"And I remember that my brother sat listen-
ing, eyes very bright, to spring suddenly to his feet,
boasting: 'When I am a man my feet will be fleet
as the East Wind. My body will be strong. I will
ride the wildest of wild horses and I will be the
bravest of all the Crows. I will fight for my people
against all enemies and take many scalps and make
coup and become a chief.'

"Many snows passed swiftly," Plenty Coups
went on, "four—six—eight—until I was a big boy
—so high. And my body, though slender, was very
strong—strong like the slender string of the bow
that sends the arrow singing far up into the Blue.
And now, when the warriors returned from battle
and danced around the camp fire I no longer fell
asleep by my mother's side. Instead, I sat erect
and listened to the stories of the brave ones, of how
they took picketed horses from the camps of their
enemies and also enemy scalps.

"As I listened the blood ran hot in my veins.

I learned that the Crows were the swiftest of all
runners, the bravest of all warriors, and the strongest of all men. And I burned to be like them, swift
and strong and brave.

"I remember the day my brother first sat me on
a horse. I was only four snows old, then. The horse
was gentle. He fastened a thong to one of my feet,
passed it under the belly of the horse, and tied it to
the other foot, so, no matter how frightened I became, I could not fall off. Then he struck the horse
and it galloped back and forth over the plains near
our camp. I was not frightened. My heart was
singing with pride. I shouted to my mother to see
how well I could ride.

"I have always loved horses," Plenty Coups
mused. "I look into their eyes and speak to them
and they understand what I say. I believe the Indian understands the language of a horse better
than the white man does. I love dogs, too. I have
never been without a dog.

"We ran races, we Crow boys, my brother and
myself and all the rest. Often the safety of a camp
depends upon its fleet-footed runners. Each day
we boys ran swifter and longer. We chased butterflies and caught them and smeared their wings upon
our chests because the women told us to do that
would soon make us as fast as butterflies. The wise
women knew better, of course, but thus, even in
our play, they prepared us for life.

"I wished to run very fast—faster than any of

the boys. I went off into a clearing across the creek and ran, ran so swiftly that the wind sang past my ears. It seemed to me that my feet were like flying birds. Yet, in the races, other boys were faster than I.

"Our mothers marked off a race track for us, and every day, while they watched, each mother hoping her son would win, we raced. And, though I had caught many butterflies and smeared them on my chest, and though I ran alone day by day, more and more swiftly, yet, in the races there were always other boys fleeter than I. So, while other mothers smiled with pride, I crept to my mother's side, head lowered, burning with shame.

"She said nothing. She smiled, and I did not then understand the meaning of her smile. But the next day, when the races were about to start, my mother suddenly spoke: 'Today our boys shall run a longer race. We will put the goal mark farther away.'

"For my mother understood that while I could never win in a short dash, I had more power of endurance than the other boys and might win in a long race.

"So, with our toes on the line drawn in the dust, we stood ready, and when the women gave the sign, we ran. For the first hundred yards I, as usual, was behind. Then one of the swiftest runners dropped out, his heart pounding like the heart of a frightened elk, then another, and another.

But I ran on and on, my body unwearied, my feet like birds' wings. And I won the race."

Plenty Coups went on, as he and Doc Allen lay beside the camp fire, smoking: "I trotted back to camp, breathing naturally, not weary at all. My mother smiled. The warriors eyed me with pride. I knew they were thinking it was good that the Crows should have in their tribe a young man who could run swiftly very long distances without tiring, for often our wolves, scouting on mountain peaks, two—three—sleeps away, had need of runners to carry messages back to camp, down steep mountain sides, or along deep cañons where horses could not travel.

"And now, all day long my heart sings. White Eagle knows how it is when a boy is young and his sinews are strong and the stream of life flows fast within him so that he wants to leap and run like a wild colt. And White Eagle knows how it is when a boy has done something that makes his mother proud and causes the brave warriors to speak well of him."

Doc Allen refilled his pipe and lit it with a glowing stick from the fire. "Yes," he said, "I know."

"Next," Plenty Coups continued, "I learned to swim. My brother and my uncle taught me. They threw me far out into the stream and left me to sink or to splash my way to shore as best I could. And I did splash. I knew they were not far away

and would come if I called for help. But, though
I was frightened, I did not call. I splashed and
choked and sank and rose again and managed to
reach the shore alone. After that I was never
afraid of water. Soon I could swim swiftly, as
swiftly as most of the boys. But—" Plenty
Coups paused and stared gravely into the fire.
"But White Eagle knows that always I have desired
to be not only as good as the best, but the best.

"I watched the beaver swim. I perceived that
I swam, not easily and steadily like him, but with a
great splashing and churning of my arms in the
water that wasted my strength. I knew that I had
not found the right way. So, while other boys
played, I went alone to the river and lay for hours
on the bank, hidden in the tall grasses, very still,
and watched the beaver as it shot swiftly through
the water. I observed that the animal was fast because it made no waste motions. I believed that it
gained its momentum by means of its wide, webbed
hind foot with which it paddled itself forward. So,
lying there, I thought foolish boy thoughts.

" 'If I catch a beaver,' I said to myself, 'and
kill it and cut off its two hind feet and spread out
the webs and tie them to my own feet, then I shall
swim very fast, like the beaver.' "

Plenty Coups chuckled at his boyish pranks as
he went on: "So I killed a beaver and cut off its
hind feet and spread out the webs until they were
wide. Then, when no one saw me, I tied them to

my feet with antelope thongs and leaped back into the water. But still I did not swim as fast as the beaver—not much faster than before. My heart was tired and heavy and I went to my mother. I said to her: 'I wish to learn to swim very fast, for soon our swimming races will begin. But, although I have tied beaver webs to my feet, I do not swim fast enough.'

"She listened to me and did not smile. Even when I showed her the webs tied to my feet she did not smile. She said to me: 'I will help you.'

"And, though she had no faith in the webs, she took them and punched holes in them, one for each toe. Then, with thongs, she tied them to my feet so they could not slip. Now my heart was singing again. Day after day I ran, alone, to the swimming hole. There I tried with the webs on my feet, and each day I became a better swimmer. I thought it was because of the web stretched across my feet. I thought the beaver was my strong medicine. I did not understand then what my mother knew, that it was only because I worked hard while the other boys played that I was becoming a good swimmer.

"Still I was not satisfied. I studied the frog and learned that it kicked its legs straight back instead of splashing with knee and foot, as I had been doing. So I tried the motion of the frog, then back onto the bank to watch, and down into the water to try again.

"Three more sleeps and the day of the great

swimming race came. All the camp was excited. Many of the great hunters and warriors stood on the river bank to watch. Through the crowd I saw my mother look at me and smile. She and I alone knew the secret of the web feet. Carefully, that day she had tied them to my feet.

" 'Go cover your feet with mud so the webs cannot be seen,' she said. 'Then, when the race is over, when you have won, while all are excited, put your moccasins on quickly, that none may know of your strong medicine.'

"At the words of my mother my heart sang. I knew then I was going to win. The night before, while sleep was upon all the lodges, while the Old Woman was shining bright upon the water, I went out alone to swim, with the beaver webs on my feet. Soon I saw a big bachelor beaver rise to the top of the water and start across. I slid softly into the river and swam after him. The Old Woman made everything very bright. The beaver went smoothly, swiftly ahead. Silently, swiftly I swam after him, faster and faster. I gained upon him. Now he was ten yards ahead of me, now five, now I could have reached out my hand and touched him. And now he looked around and saw me and made for his hole under the willows. He swam very fast. I was just behind him and then I was beside him. I thrust out my hand to seize him.

" 'I will take him back to camp,' I thought, 'and show all the people that I have done what no other boy has ever done—caught a bachelor beaver in a swimming race.'

"But just then he whacked the water with his broad tail and shot beneath the willows. Though I did not capture the beaver I had beaten him in our swimming race, so now I knew I could win against the boys. And I did just as my mother told me to do, and I did win.

"When I climbed onto the bank far ahead of the other boys I slipped my feet quickly into the moccasins my mother held for me there. And the old warriors looked at me and I walked straight and proud for I knew they were thinking, 'He is a Crow brave, swift and strong. It is such boys that grow up to be great warriors.'

"And then, for the first time the thought came to me almost as though someone were speaking the words aloud: 'Some day you may be chief of your people.' "

Plenty Coups got to his feet. "I have hunted and eaten and smoked with my paleface brother, White Eagle," he said. "I have told him much of my boyhood days. Now I am rested and I go on to my lodge. Some time, when we meet again, I will tell him more."

Plenty Coups shook hands with Allen, got on his horse and rode away. Doctor Allen watched him, a slender, strong, straight figure, until he was a part of the shadows of the moonlit prairie.

Left alone, Allen stirred the embers of the fire,

took out notebook and pencil, and wrote down all the young Crow brave had told him, for it is seldom an Indian opens his heart to a white man. That entry in his journal Dr. Allen has dated August, 1881.

Plenty Coups, chief of all the tribes of the Northwest, a shrunken, feeble old man of eighty-three snows, almost blind, still laughs heartily as he recalls the story of the time so many moons ago when he was young and strong and full of life, and when to be the swiftest runner and the swiftest swimmer seemed to him matters of vast import. And they were important.

That same ambitious and adventurous spirit, that same staunch perseverance, had he chanced to be born of another race, might have made of him a second Caesar or Napoleon or Lincoln. He had within him the qualities that tend toward greatness. Always he wanted to be "not only as good as the best, but the best."

The super-abounding energy and urge to excel which spurred him on in every youthful undertaking was, years later, after many harrowing experiences, to make of him a chief, beloved and reverenced by his people, loved and respected by the whites. Today, within that shriveled, tottering, blinded figure is still the spark of power which holds to him the loyalty of his subjects.

They watch over him tenderly, the young men of the tribe, although they might so easily take advantage of his helpless old age and usurp the position of dignity which he has won. Perhaps, in the hearts of the Crows, there remains something of the pagan's tendency toward hero-worship. Unquestionably in their eyes the old chief is a hero. It is to their credit that these copper-skinned pagans do not forget what they owe him in loyalty and gratitude.

They realize that he has guided them wisely, cautiously, with far-sighted vision, through that inevitably difficult period of adjustment when a conquered race bows to the mandates of its conquerors. Many times he has journeyed to Washington, struggling desperately to keep for his tribe some portion of the land they love and he has proved himself an able statesman and a shrewd diplomat.

He has witnessed the invasion of the whites into the plains of the buffalo, that earthly paradise of the red man. He has viewed the ruthless undermining of all the tribal habits and customs and traditions that seemed to him and his people right. He has known them to be mocked and ridiculed, those customs and habits and traditions which seem sacred to the Indian, all bound up within his heart as they are by unwritten ages of conflict and achievement, of hope and despair, of love and hate. And yet, hiding his own grief and bitterness, he has, through the difficult years, preached to his young men, hot-headed, rebellious, proud, not only a physical but a spiritual surrender.

"This is no longer the land of the Indian," he says to them. "It is the land of the white man. Those of you who are wise will become educated in the white man's school, adopt the white man's ways, work hard on your farms with your horses and make of yourselves good farmers and good men. But I would have you cling to the memories of your fathers. I would have you still go up onto the mountain and see visions so that your hearts may be clean and strong. The day of the warrior is past. This is an age, not of the war club, but of the plow."

So speaks old Chief Plenty Coups to his young men today, even while the dark shadows are gathering thick over his head. And they listen, those of them who are wise, for they know that an Indian chief has never been made. They know he makes himself. They know Plenty Coups is their chief because, and only because, he has proved his courage in battle, his fortitude in situations that try the very heart of man, his physical and soul capacity to lead and govern others. The Crows understand nothing of political pull or propaganda or corruption, of scheming and lying for votes. In their pagan simplicity they hold that the man who would be chief must first prove his ability to rule. He must be a "kon-ning," a man that knows or can.

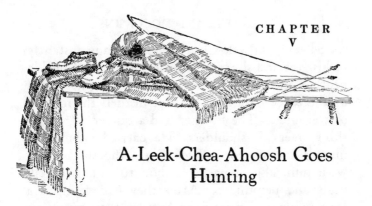

A-Leek-Chea-Ahoosh Goes Hunting

A-LEEK-CHEA-AHOOSH felt someone giving him a poke in the ribs. He grunted indignantly and yawned and turned over on his bed of buffalo robes to go back to sleep. It was still very early in the morning and his eyes refused to open. But again came that poking finger. Looking up, he saw his big brother bending over him and recalled their plans for the day.

The night before, while their uncle and other warriors of the Crows were gathered around the fire in the tepee, smoking and talking about wars they had fought with the Blackfeet, A-Leek-Chea-Ahoosh and his big brother lay curled close together on a buffalo robe in a far corner of the tepee. They had talked in whispers so as not to disturb the old ones. They had planned that in the morning, very early, they would go out into the woods hunting, like the brave hunters of their tribe. For they desired in all things to be like grown men, strong and fearless.

So now A-Leek-Chea-Ahoosh sprang instantly
to his feet and slipped his hand into that of his big
brother and together the two stole so quietly out
of the tepee that they did not disturb the mother
or the uncle. The brother had a quiver of arrows
slung over his shoulders. He carried a bow for
himself and one for A-Leek-Chea-Ahoosh. He had
with him, also, a parfleche box full of dried elk
meat and pemmican. After they had tramped a
long while and were very hungry they would sit
down by the creek and eat. To the little boy he
entrusted the horsehair snare with which, during
their adventurous day, they might catch some
rabbits.

The small brother was five, then, and the older
one, ten. They visioned with the optimism of the
born hunter how they would return at night, staggering under the burden of their game, and astonish
all the camp with the evidence of their skill. They
would have birds and fish and many rabbits. All
the old men of the tribe would exclaim: "Here
come our two mighty hunters!" And their mother
would feel very proud.

Never had the beautiful land of the Crows appeared so enchanting. All along the creek the
cottonwood trees and quaking asps were ablaze
with emerald and crimson and gold. Wild rose
bushes and kinnikinnick were like splashes of fire
against mountain sides. Every leaf on the trees,
every blade of grass in the valley, sparkled with

silvery frost. The lazy sun had not yet risen, and the Old Woman looked very pale and weary up in the Blue.

The cold morning air, spicy with pine and sage-brush, set the bodies of the two boys to tingling and their blood to racing. As they crept hand-in-hand away from the sleeping camp, stepping cautiously in their moccasined feet lest a crackling twig arouse the sleepers, they chuckled with glee. They longed to whoop their joy. A-Leek-Chea-Ahoosh felt that he could run forever across vast plains like a young elk, without thought of tiring. This was his first man's escapade, his first venture away from camp without his mother.

When they returned at night she would, of course, scold them for being naughty runaways, but after she saw the many rabbits and fish they were bringing her she would laugh and call them "Little Magpies."

For an hour they stalked through thick beds of fallen leaves which rustled like music under foot, the big brother leading, the small boy trudging along behind, and frost-laden branches of under-brush along the creek whipped against them and showered frost nettles down upon them and made them laugh.

At length, after the two had been tramping about for what seemed to the little fellow long hours, he pleaded that they stop to eat. Never had he felt so hungry. The big brother laughed and pointed to the sun. It was still but a ball of red above the eastern mountains. However, they found a clearing on the banks of Mission Creek, under a golden spread of cottonwoods, and opened their parfleche box and ate strips of delicious dried elk meat and pemmican. No breakfast in their whole lives had ever tasted so good. When they had eaten sparingly, for hunters and warriors do not gorge themselves, they lay flat on their stomachs and drank of the icy water of the creek.

While they were drinking they saw, down on the creek bottom through the clear water, a speckled trout. It was a big fish. It seemed to them the biggest fish they had ever seen. For a long time, with the horsehair snare, they endeavored to catch it. The boys were patient but the trout was wary. Each time it evaded the noose just as they were ready to draw it tight. Nevertheless they did not give up until, with a saucy flirt of its tail, it swam away out of sight.

A beaver dam extended from the bank out into the water, and the boys caught sight of a big bachelor beaver swimming swiftly through the water toward it. Now, indeed, they were incited to action. Their eyes shone; their cheeks burned. The big brother, breathing hard, got ready his bow and arrow and took careful aim while A-Leek-Chea-Ahoosh danced about on frenzied feet. To catch a bachelor beaver! To carry it into camp and sling it down at their mother's feet! That would most certainly prove them able hunters, for beavers are fair game for grown men, very hard to hit.

The beaver, fat and fluffy, sailed along, with a smack of its broad tail on the water. The brother sent his arrow down but it was just a hair's breadth away. The animal disappeared. For a long time they watched to see if drops of blood showed on the water's surface, but none came up. They had missed and the beaver was safe.

"If we had had a bull-boat," the brother said, "we could have followed him and caught him. When we return we will ask our mother for a bull-boat and she will make one for us."

Just then a flock of blackbirds, chattering loudly, passed over their heads on their way south, so many that they blackened air and sky. The big brother sent an arrow up into the gabbling, coal-black mass and down came a bird at the very feet of A-Leek-Chea-Ahoosh. The small boy was proud. No skilled hunter bringing down a swift buffalo on the run could have felt more exultant. He strung the kill on a willow twig and slung it over his shoulder.

"This, the blackbird," he announced, gravely, "will be my strong medicine."

The brother did not hear him. He was gazing across a valley and up onto mountains rose-tinted by the morning sun. For miles and miles, much farther than eye could see, all that wide valley

along the Echeta Casha and the mountains from
Mission Creek to Absarokee and south to Pryor was
Crow land. Down on the plains where grass grew
tall and thick grazed millions of buffalo and wild
horses. Up on the mountains were elk and deer
and bear and sheep. All—all belonged to the
Crow people. It was theirs by right of the purchase
price of suffering and bloodshed.

A mute rapture welled up within the heart of
the young patriot as he paused to view this land of
his fathers. He was deeply moved. He felt an
acute and passionate longing to prove his devotion
to his country, even, if need be, by the giving of his
life.

But A-Leek-Chea-Ahoosh's impatient hand was
tugging at his arm, recalling him to the present,
and his moment of exaltation vanished.

"I see a rabbit," the small boy was shouting.
"Under that kinnikinnick."

They chased the rabbit. It would be a great
thing to catch it alive and take it home as a pet.
But the cottontail, really not at all frightened, loped
easily along just ahead, pausing now and then to
cast interested glances back upon its breathless,
excited pursuers. It led them along creek banks
and down coulees and through underbrush that
caught and scratched, and finally, when they felt
they could not run another step, it scurried down
its hole to safety.

For a long time the boys, patient, alert, lay

close to that hole, noose ready to snare it when it came out. Often Indian boys did catch rabbits with horsehair snares. But this particular rabbit had either sought another exit or had fallen into a comfortable snooze down in its subterranean home. At all events it kept them waiting so long that A-Leek-Chea-Ahoosh also began to nod and blink sleepily. After all, he was but five snows old, the valiant little hunter, and the day had been long and full of exciting adventures.

So the big brother pulled the small lad down beside him on a bed of leaves and cuddled him close, as their mother would have done, and gave him of the dried elk meat. Soon the weary head nodded and the dark eyes closed.

When he wakened, the sun was dropping behind the western peaks. Dusk had settled upon the woods, and small birds in the treetops were chattering drowsily. All about were small, soft, murmuring voices, the voices of the forest children, chipmunk and squirrel and rabbit, running water, wind in the trees, leaves breaking loose from parent branches and pattering down like raindrops.

"We will go to our mother," the big brother said. His arm was stiff, and ached from having held so long the sleepy head of A-Leek-Chea-Ahoosh.

Tired and guilty, clothing torn, faces and hands scratched, the two hunters returned to their village, they who had started out in the morning with such high hopes. They knew that their anxious mother would have worried about them all the day, fearing that some prowling Sioux or Blackfeet had stolen her sons. She would scold them and they would have nothing but the one blackbird to lay at her feet as justification for their naughtiness.

No one, however, noticed them. Throughout the village there was bustle and noise and confusion. The very air was full of excitement. Women were rushing about, sorting belongings and packing them on travois, bringing in pack horses, talking and laughing as they worked.

A-Leek-Chea-Ahoosh found his mother in their tepee packing beaded moccasins and belts and headbands—all the beautiful things she had made by the light of the fire, evenings, while warriors talked—packing them in large parfleche boxes that were to be tied to the sides of horses. He showed her the limp little blackbird and she did not scold. She took it and said: "Some day you will be a mighty hunter and will bring to our tepee much buffalo meat, and many bear and elk teeth. Lie down and rest now, for soon we travel the dark trail. While the Old Woman is yet up in the Blue the whole village is moving. We will travel many sleeps and go to live on the banks of the Echeta Casha."

"Why?" A-Leek-Chea-Ahoosh demanded.

"It is not for women and children to understand," his mother answered, sternly. "It has something to do with a treaty between our wise men

A Crow Meercotty. Photograph by Goff.

Crow papooses in gala attire. Photograph by Dr. Allen.

and the palefaces. I only know that we must
move."

"And we wish," said the big brother, "that
there you would make for us a bull-boat. Then we
can catch for you many beaver so you need never
fear hunger nor cold."

To the boys the country along the Echeta Casha
seemed very much like the country they had left.
Here, also, there were wide, grassy valleys and cold
streams rushing down from the mountains and
thickets of plum trees and chokecherry and bull-
berry bushes. Together the two explored the woods
and became one with the small woods-children.
Soon they discovered where wild honey trees were,
and beaver dams and deep swimming holes and
dark pools where speckled trout played. They
mocked bird voices and the wolf howl. They
chased rabbits into holes and helped their mother
gather berries for winter pemmican. They helped
her scrape buffalo hides that their uncle brought
in from the kill, and beat them soft and tan them
for robes.

The mother said: "It is going to be a long, cold
winter. All the wise wood-creatures are telling us
that. See! The bees are storing their honey high
up in trees, away from deep snows. The beavers
are filling their houses with food. We will be wise.
We will gather many berries and much honey. We
will dry much elk meat and buffalo meat and many
buffalo tongues. Then we will not fear winter
snows."

The boys had moccasins lined with fur and buffalo robes made with the fur side in. They did not fear the winter. When snows covered the mountain sides and every twig of tree and bush snapped with cold and even the rushing waters of the Echeta Casha were frozen over, then short winter days were not long enough for all they wished to do. From morning till night they were busy with sleds and skates and skiis.

All too soon, so it seemed to them, spring suns melted ice and snow; buds came out on the bushes; in the low places grass showed green, and every dry run was filled with water that sang its song as it went leaping down to the plains.

Then the big brother said again to his mother: "We wish a bull-boat so we can go smoothly over the water as the wild duck goes."

She set about making them a boat, and they helped her, excited and happy. She took the largest of the buffalo hides which their uncle had brought in from the hunt and together she and the boys stretched it over hoops made of tough willow. The boys cut slender willow branches and scorched them over a fire to toughen them still more. These she bound to the edge of the hide, sewing them with antelope thongs so that when dried the whole would become as strong as iron, and round, like a cup. Finally she and her sons rubbed tallow on the outside of the cup-shaped boat, rubbed it in and pounded it in until the hide was waterproof. And how the boys did work those days! Never, now, need their mother scold them because they ran off into the woods to play when she wanted fuel for her fire or an elk-hide bag of water. They begrudged the time spent eating and sleeping, so impatient were they for the boat to be finished.

And because the boys wanted the most beautiful boat of all the Crows, their mother left the tail and head of the buffalo on the boat, taking great pains to stuff the head carefully. And the head was to be the prow of the boat, the tail was to be the stern.

There followed long, agonized days of waiting, while the hide must be left to dry in the sun, before it was pronounced waterproof and safe. But at last, after a restless night in which sleep was all mixed up with dreams of wild adventures on the water, the momentous morning came. Triumphantly A-Leek-Chea-Ahoosh and his brother carried their boat down to the river and, while many boys stood on the bank watching with envious eyes, they launched it.

The famous Chief Plenty Coups has had many high moments in his eventful life, but doubtless none so surcharged with exultant pride and joy as that moment when he stepped into the boat beside his brother and went dancing, light as a bubble, down the rapid stream.

There followed for the two brothers joyous, carefree spring days, when they navigated their

boat over miniature rapids and around sharp
curves, sometimes successfully, often with more
or less discomforting mishaps. They loved to sit
idle, allowing their boat to drift slowly along on
quiet streams shaded by cottonwoods, between
banks that were green with moist, moss-covered
stones and with ferns, while over them always
hung the silent, brooding mountains, like a watchful mother, guarding them.

The irresponsible delight of those days sank
deep into the heart of the boy who was destined
later to take upon himself the perplexities and
troubles of his tribe. Perhaps the memories of that
happy time are etched the more sharply upon his
consciousness because they mark the last of the gay
camaraderie between himself and the brother he
loved.

Soon the five years' difference in their ages began to separate them. While A-Leek-Chea-Ahoosh
was still a little boy, thinking a child's thoughts,
content to spend all his hours in play, the brother
was beginning to stir under the prick of a man's
thoughts and a man's ambitions. The age of
puberty was upon him and he took long strides
away from the clinging, lonely lad.

Plenty Coups remembers with what mingled
pride and dread he watched his brother leave the
village, alone, and stride across the plains toward
the mountains on his way to the summit where he
must remain till visions came to him and he re-

ceived his strong medicine. A-Leek-Chea-Ahoosh
stood watching his brother, a tall, slim boy of
eighteen, as he grew smaller and smaller far out on
the plains, became a speck against the mountain
and then was lost in its shadows. When he returned—if he did return, for some boys died of
hunger and exhaustion up there in that high mysterious Blue—he would be a man, ready to take up
the duties and responsibilities of the warrior, and
A-Leek-Chea-Ahoosh must renounce his playmate
forever.

Plenty Coups remembers how, after many
sleeps, men went up onto the mountain and returned, bearing between them the brother, pale and
weak from hunger and thirst, his eyes shining
from an inner glory. Then there were council
meetings of the medicine men to which A-Leek-
Chea-Ahoosh was not admitted, when the brother
recounted his experiences, his dreams and visions,
and told of the strong medicine that had come to
him, and waited, anxiously, for the medicine man's
interpretation.

Shortly after that the Crow chief, Pretty Eagle,
sent a crier through the village calling all the warriors and headmen to a council meeting. Later
there was an open meeting. Close around the camp
fire sat warriors and headmen and medicine men,
wolves and runners, all the officials of the tribe, and
in that circle sat the big brother, wearing the
honors of man's estate proudly. Farther away, in

an outer circle, were squaws and children. And A-Leek-Chea-Ahoosh, sitting beside his mother, heard Pretty Eagle say, "The Sioux come many times to our land to kill our buffalo. That is well. Buffalo in our hunting ground are like stars in the Blue. While we have plenty, squaws and papooses of other tribes must not suffer hunger. But our enemy not only kill our buffalo, they also steal our horses. And they say because we do nothing we are not braves. They say we, the Crows, have hearts like squaws. Our wolves have seen smoke from Sioux camps on Blue Creek. Who of our young men will go into the enemy camp and recover our horses?"

Plenty Coups remembers that it was his brother who sprang first to his feet, saying, "My heart is strong. My arrows fly swift and straight. I will lead our young men to our enemy's camp and will recover the horses of the Crows."

And so, next morning, before the sun showed red above eastern mountains, the brother of A-Leek-Chea-Ahoosh started south toward Blue Creek, leading a band of twenty young warriors. Sitting their horses proudly, quivers slung across their shoulders, bows in hand, ready for the enemy, they went out from the village, brave of heart, singing Crow war songs.

It seemed to the small boy watching the riders as far as he could see that his brother, leading the Crow warriors, was far more fearless and tall and strong and splendid than any other young brave. And the heart of the boy sang with pride and love.

Six sleeps the people of the Crow village waited for news of their young men. Every morning and many times during the day wolves climbed lookout peaks to gaze far across the valley for a glimpse of them. Very early on the seventh morning Pretty Eagle glanced up to the peak and saw a spiral of smoke curling toward the Blue, not steadily, but in puffs—short, long—short, short—long, short. By means of blanket and fire a wolf was telegraphing the news that warriors were returning, bringing many horses. Immediately a crier was dispatched to spread the tidings throughout the village.

Then preparations were made for a feast and dance. Children gathered piles of wood and brought it into the village, and squaws built fires that leaped up into the treetops, and cooked big kettles of buffalo meat. Meanwhile all the men— the medicine men and headmen and old warriors and boys—leaped onto their horses and raced far out across the plains to welcome the returning victors. All eyes could see them now, with their big band of horses.

A-Leek-Chea-Ahoosh rode out with the others, his heart bursting with impatience and joy. His brother would be a great warrior. Perhaps he had made coup and was bringing back many Sioux scalps to hang on the scalp pole. Soon, because he was so brave, he would be a great chief.

But the returning warriors were not wearing their feathered war bonnets. They were not giving their war cries, nor waving war clubs and toma-hawks. They were approaching silently, and with drooping heads. A-Leek-Chea-Ahoosh understood what that meant. Though they had conquered the enemy and recaptured Crow horses yet it had not been without loss of life. Some one of their own had fallen by an enemy arrow. So tonight, instead of rejoicing in the Crow village, there would be the beat of muffled drums and the wail of a bereaved mother and the crooning death song of the women.

A-Leek-Chea-Ahoosh struck his pony with a quirt and hurried on. He looked, drew nearer and looked again, and now, although he could see the faces of the warriors plainly, he could not see his brother's face. He was not at the head of the braves nor anywhere in their midst. Twenty young men had gone out to vindicate the courage of the Crow people, and nineteen had returned. The valiant brother of A-Leek-Chea-Ahoosh had been killed by the Sioux.

Grief tore at the heart of the boy, and hatred and anger. Silently he swore to himself a vow. Soon he would be a man and then he would not rest until he had gone into the very camp of the Sioux and had killed one of their warriors—per-haps the greatest of all the Sioux—to avenge his brother's death.

That night there was wailing and mourning in the Crow village for their young brave who had fallen at enemy hands. The mother painted her face black and sat huddled on the ground, swaying, weeping; and other mothers, knowing how grief was chilling her heart, wept with her. All through the long dark hours of the night the cries of the women stirred the stillness. Drums beat a low, muffled tom-tom. The braves danced around the fire, chanting war songs and death songs, recounting how they had met the enemy, how bravely their comrade had fought, and how he had died.

A-Leek-Chea-Ahoosh could not bear it. He crept into the tepee and flung himself down, but it was lonely there and soon he was up again, wandering out into the thick darkness of the woods. He felt his way to the bank of the creek and lay prone on the ground, his young limbs heavy and weary with grief. From far away, through the black silence, drifted the beat of the drums. He ached with loneliness. He gazed up at the mountains and felt their comforting presence entering into him. He stared up into the Blue, wondering if his brother were already there, somewhere in that vast, still mystery, happy and well. The creek went tinkling along, and up and down on its waves the bull-boat danced.

Suddenly the boy leaped to his feet and went groping for stones. He began hacking at the boat, pounding and pounding it until there were big holes in it and water crept in and it started to sink. Slowly the boat sank down, and the boy stood watching until water had completely covered it. Never again would it go bounding merrily over the waves. For his brother he had made the greatest sacrifice in his power, he had given up the thing he loved best. Now there remained to him, when he became a man, the taking of the life of a Sioux, to avenge his brother's death.

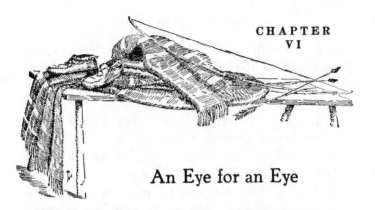

An Eye for an Eye

AFTER the death of his brother many snows
passed swiftly. A-Leek-Chea-Ahoosh did all
the things Crow boys were accustomed to do—
laughed and sang, raced and wrestled, fished and
hunted, grew strong of heart and sinew, lived his
small child-tragedies and his joys. But rushing
years, though they dulled the first acute pang, did
not obliterate his loneliness, merely covered it over.
Often the voices of the woods and the creek and
the mountains spoke to him of his brother.

He had one close friend, Big Shoulders, a boy
of his own age. To him he spoke of the emptiness
of his heart and of how he meant sometime to seek
revenge. The fixed purpose colored his thoughts
and all that he did. Even in his play, now, while
he was wrestling he was thinking, "This will make
my muscles strong." Or, when he was running
foot-races across the plains, "This will teach me
endurance." Or, when he shot at targets, "I am
learning to be sure with eye and hand. Some day

my target shall be the heart of a Sioux." And there
was a steady, determined flash of his bright eyes,
an expression thoughtful and sober beyond his
years, on his young face.

The day came for A-Leek-Chea-Ahoosh to go
up onto the mountain as his brother had done, to
fast in solitude and receive his strong medicine.
Three days, without food or water, he remained
up there in the vast blue stillness. When he was
very weak, so weak that he thought he was going
to die, he lay on a rock, while the sun poured its
merciless heat down upon him, and then frag-
mentary dreams, beautiful visions, came to him,
and voices spoke to him. He thought that an eagle,
swiftest and bravest and strongest of birds, floated
over him and spoke to him. He thought the eagle
lifted him in strong talons and bore him far up into
the Blue, and then safely down the mountain and
back to his people. And A-Leek-Chea-Ahoosh
knew the eagle to be his strong medicine. He knew
that nothing could ever harm him, for the eagle
would be with him in danger all his life, to guard
him.

Soon after that, at the time when elk were rub-
bing velvet from their antlers on the quaking asps,
A-Leek-Chea-Ahoosh spoke gravely to his friend
Big Shoulders. "Today while I was out on the
plains an eagle circled over my head, very close. I
know by that that the hour has come. After one
more sleep I will travel the dark trail until I reach

the camp of the Sioux and there I will kill a Sioux, perhaps the bravest warrior of all the Sioux, so that my brother's death may be avenged. I have spoken."

Big Shoulders replied, "I know that our enemy are killing buffalo for their winter's meat and are camped on the Musselshell beyond the Echeta Casha Asha. Your grief is my grief, your dangers shall be my dangers. I will go with you."

"Your heart speaks," A-Leek-Chea-Ahoosh said. "We will tell no one of our mission. We will make ready for our journey and, after one sleep, when the Old Woman is bright in the Blue, we will start. We shall travel many sleeps."

So, when no one saw them, the boys went out onto the plains and caught their horses and picketed them close to the village in a cottonwood thicket. Secretly they filled parfleche boxes with meat and tied them onto the horses. They filled quivers with many arrows. Then, the next night, when all the camp was asleep, they stole quietly away.

All that night they journeyed, riding slowly at first, while the horses' stomachs were full of grass and water, then faster. They came to Clarks Fork and followed it down to its junction with the Yellowstone River. By that time the sun was high in the Blue and they dared ride no longer across the open plains, for they were approaching enemy country where at any moment from lookout peaks the sharp eyes of enemy wolves might spy them.

So they rode their horses down into a cañon

winding between high hills where it was cool and
dark. Down there, in basins of rock, they found
pools of water left from fall rains. Stripping bark
from cottonwood trees they fed their horses. They
themselves, though they were hungry, ate sparingly of the dried elk meat in their parfleche boxes, for
they knew not how many sleeps they might have
to travel. Then, while one boy watched, the other
slept. But instantly, at the faintest sound from
above, the louder swish of pine trees, the crackling
of a twig or crunch of a stone under foot of a wild
animal, they were awake and alert, breath hushed,
creeping up to the lip of the cañon to peer out
across sun-bathed plains for signs of prowling
Sioux.

From time to time during their long day's vigil
they crawled, stomachs flat to the ground, up a
high butte from where they could see all the wide
valley of the Yellowstone, its buttes and rolling
hills and rivers and dry runs, as far as the Crazy
Mountains and the Beartooths and the Pryors, but
they saw no signs of the enemy, no life at all except
slowly moving specks here and there that sharp
young eyes told them were bands of wild horses
and buffalo.

After the sun had slipped down behind rimrocks, and long shadows from butte and hill were
spreading out across the plains the boys again ate
and then, rested and refreshed and tingling with
the thrill of adventure, followed the dark trail

along the banks of the Yellowstone toward Hoskin
and McGirl's trading post, where Huntley now
stands. They rode as fast as they dared, over plains
gutted with deep cañons into which a rider might
plunge, and pricked with countless prairie-dog
holes in which a horse might break its leg.

Early the second morning they reached Huntley and there once more they camped, hidden in a
coulee, resting through the day. The second night
they crossed the hills to Musselshell River. Somewhere along the banks of this river they knew the
Sioux to be camped. Following the stream they
came, presently, to a bend from where the valley
widened. Here it was covered with tall, thick
grass and dotted with groves of frost-yellowed
cottonwood and gorged this way and that by dry
runs and ravines. Here there were many rock-
ribbed, pine-tipped buttes offering service as lookout peaks.

In the breasts of the two Crow boys excitement
burned. Their breath came fast and hard. When
they spoke it was in low, jerky, rasping whispers.
Their bodies trembled, but not from fear, or if so,
from a rather pleasurable, stimulating fear. This,
their first adventure, was fraught with genuine
peril. They were alone, more than a hundred miles
from their own people, in the country of an enemy
who would be glad to kill them upon sight. From
behind any one of those thickets or buttes might
at any moment come whining an enemy's arrow,

aimed at their thudding hearts. And they did not desire death. Life was all before them, mysterious and beautiful. But they had been trained to the habits and thoughts and emotions of the warrior every hour of whose life must be threatened by death. To make coup, prove his courage and fortitude, raise himself to a position of distinction in the social life of his people, is the burning ambition of every Indian boy. From the first lullaby their mothers had crooned to them and on through boyhood these two had been taught that fear is only for squaws. Years later, when A-Leek-Chea-Ahoosh had become the old Chief Plenty Coups, he was to say before a large assembly of whites gathered in front of his log house out on Pryor: "My people have ever been fighting men, and I believe the warrior ranks highest among all the professions. He fights for his women, his children, and his home. Therefore, Chief War Eagle, my heart goes out to you because you too are a great warrior who has done great service for our country."

But the boy A-Leek-Chea-Ahoosh, some sixty years before he made that speech, could not still the fast beating of his heart as he and Big Shoulders went prowling through enemy country on their first war raid. Having concealed their horses in a thicket close to the river they had crawled up onto a butte to reconnoiter. At first they could see nothing but buffalo and horses. For a long time,

with the watchful patience of wolves, they lay
sprawled under pine trees on their lookout peak,
scrutinizing the valley below. Finally A-Leek-
Chea-Ahoosh whispered, "Look!" and pointed to a
black moving mass some ten miles away. "Look!
Buffalo!"

Buffalo, but not, as they noted at once, grazing
peacefully, undisturbed. The animals were milling
about uneasily as though they scented danger.

"The Sioux! Out for their winter meat."

Quickly they scrambled down the sides of the
butte. Two lads, neither over twenty, courage and
skill untried, about to invade the hunting camp of
the Sioux, fiercest of all Crow enemies. They made
a wild dash across the plains to their horses. Although they were separated from the Sioux by ten
miles, if they could see the enemy, so might the
enemy see them. Indians are seldom without wolves
on lookout peaks.

All that day the boys lay under cottonwood
trees, eating the last of their dried elk meat, speaking in whispers, one watching vigilantly while the
other dozed, both waiting impatiently for the sun
to go down. It was a long day for them. They discussed various plans of attack and longed for the
heads of wise men. Should they walk or ride the
last ten miles? Should they dash furiously into the
very midst of the Sioux hunters, giving their war
cries, brandishing war clubs, quite as though there
were back of them countless numbers of Crow
braves? That appealed to them as being wildly

venturesome and courageous. What tales they could tell as they danced round the Crow scalp pole! However, they decided against it, knowing that warriors, though brave, are always cautious, never foolish. And A-Leek-Chea-Ahoosh had a mission to perform. He must not fail. That vow he had made many snows ago when he hacked holes in the bull-boat and watched it submerge must be kept.

Night came and they started on the last leg of their journey toward the Sioux hunting camp. For an hour or so they jogged along slowly, hearing nothing except the sleepy night voices of the wild children of the wood and the muffled thud of their own horses' feet on thick, crisp grass. The moon rose, pricking out each butte and hill, each lone pine and bush, each cactus and soapweed, with pale silver. Then the weird, gray half-light of morning spread over everything, and with it, life on the plains began to stir.

A-Leek-Chea-Ahoosh jumped off his horse and put his ear to the ground, as he had done often during the night. Now, at last, he could hear a low, steady rumble, feel a rhythmic vibration.

"We are near," he whispered. His eyes shone bright, his breath came fast. He felt of the quiver of arrows across his shoulders, made sure his knife was in his belt, grasped his war club more tightly. "Let us picket our horses in the bottom of the draw where they cannot be seen."

There was neither tree nor bush in that dry run to which they might picket their horses, so with hunting knives they dug holes a foot deep in the pebbly bottom, laid halter ropes across and covered them over with dirt. Thus their horses were quite as securely tied as though they had been chained to an iron bar.

On foot the boys crept along down the dry run, hidden by its high banks. Presently the rumble made by the hoofs of countless animals grew louder, and they could hear the yell of men, the grunt of hunted buffalo, and now even the sharp whine of arrows.

Just ahead the banks lowered, the draw ran out into the open, into Sioux hunting ground, where there were no friendly buttes or bushes behind which to hide.

The boys got down on hands and knees and slithered their way to the mouth of the draw. There they lay flat, very still, watching the Sioux hunters out on the plains circling buffalo, closing in on them, shooting arrows into the milling mass. They could hear the panting of tired buffalo ponies, the thud-thud of their small, flying hoofs, the grunt, and then the moan of a dying buffalo or gored horse.

Lying so, the Crow boys were within sight of the Sioux, but the hunters, at that exciting moment, were off guard, giving no thought to prowling enemies. An arrow shot into that confused mass of horses and buffalo and men would be almost sure to hit a Sioux, but that would bring the whole band of hunters down upon the boys and make escape impossible. So they waited.

Watching them, A-Leek-Chea-Ahoosh was thinking, "A Sioux killed my brother. Perhaps the arrow of one of those very braves out there, heart singing with joy of the hunt, stilled my brother's heart forever."

And his hand clenched his war club. This day either he returned to his people with an enemy scalp or else his own scalp would that night be hung upon a Sioux scalp pole. It all depended upon which of His children the Great Spirit loved best—Sioux or Crow.

For long hours, with grim patience, giving no thought to food or drink, the boys crouched at the mouth of the draw—A-Leek-Chea-Ahoosh, who loved his brother, and Big Shoulders, who loved his friend. The October sun sailed high up in the Blue and sent scorching rays down upon them. They dared not move. The slightest stir, the rattle of a loose stone, a long-drawn breath, might betray their presence. Then, if the Great Spirit be merciful, a shower of poisoned arrows raining down upon them, and death. Or—far worse fate—they might be taken alive to the Sioux camp to endure the humiliations and tortures inflicted upon prisoners.

So they waited, nerves taut, watching for the providential moment when they dared send an arrow straight to the heart of one of those Sioux

braves with some hope of dashing back to their
horses and escaping.

Finally that moment arrived. A bull buffalo,
maddened by fear and agony, an arrow thrust deep
into its side, broke loose from the awful circle of
panting, sweating horses and yelling men. It shook
its big head in pain, it grunted and pawed the
earth. Its bloodshot eyes flashed desperate glances
across the wide plain, seeking a possible hiding-
place. Now it spied the ravine where the boys were
crouched and made for it, awkwardly, lumberingly,
yet with incredible speed. But now one of its
tormentors saw it and wheeled his pony in pursuit.
He would not venture an arrow at that distance
but would wait until he had caught up with it and
pierce through the shoulder down to the heart.

On they came, the wounded animal and the
Sioux hunter, lessening the distance by rods—by
yards. The Crow boys sprang to their feet, bodies
rigid, hands clutching knife and war club, in plain
view of all the hunters save that one riding to his
death with thought only for the animal ahead.
Sioux braves, after one astonished, silent moment,
shouted out a warning, but he did not heed until
it was too late. The buffalo shot past the boys and
after it came the man.

Not until he was beside them did he see them.
Then he jerked back his horse until it reared on its
haunches, and shot an arrow, then another, that
went singing past the ears of the boys. In that

instant A-Leek-Chea-Ahoosh gathered together all
the brawn of his slim lithe young body, gave a
spring, and landed upon the bewildered Sioux. The
horse plunged wildly. The Sioux snatched at his
war club, but strong arms were gripping him tight.
Big Shoulders seized the horse's head and held it.
There was a struggle, a flash of a knife in the sun,
dripping blood, and the Sioux hunter freed to go
riding back to his people, tortured head lowered in
shame. A-Leek-Chea-Ahoosh had scalped him
alive. Far more merciful to have sent an arrow
down into his heart. Never could that scalped
Sioux hope to become a warrior. He was disgraced;
he would be ostracized by his tribe, forced to wear
the dress of a squaw, and must henceforth crawl
through life in utter ignominy. The mark of the
coward was upon him, branded there, though that
he could not know, by the young brother of the
Crow brave whom the Sioux had killed on Blue
Creek years ago.

It all happened in a split second. Now the enraged Sioux, following that one breath of astonishment, were quirting their horses toward the Crows.
And the boys were speeding for their lives along
the draw toward their horses, A-Leek-Chea-Ahoosh
gripping the bloody scalp of his enemy. They
reached the horses, jerked loose the buried ropes,
and sprang onto their backs. Ensued a race through
the dry run, up steep banks, over wide plains, fifty
against two, the chances a little in favor of the

Crows, for the Sioux horses were already exhausted from the hours of the hunt.

On dashed the boys with the thunder of pursuing hoofs behind them, with Sioux yells splitting the air, with arrows whizzing past their ears. They crouched low over the horses' necks and rode like the wind. No time now to consider prairie dog holes. If a horse broke its leg, then two Crow scalps would adorn Sioux poles that night and there would be wailing and mourning in the Crow village for two of its sons that were lost.

They gained on their pursuers, came to the cottonwood thicket where they had spent the last night. There, pausing to give the horses a second's breath, they listened. No longer could they hear the thud of hoofs or the war cry of enraged Sioux. The enemy, not knowing that the two boys were alone, not knowing but that there were big bands of Crows waiting in ambush to attack them, had given up the chase.

Crow wolves on lookout peaks must have seen the returning young warriors and must have sent criers through the village with the news; for, long before A-Leek-Chea-Ahoosh and Big Shoulders were within sight of the camp, a great crowd of their people came riding out to meet them. There were grave old warriors wearing their war bonnets in honor of the heroes, hunters and braves in festive attire, gay with bright feathers and beads and jingling anklets, fat squaws on fat ponies, and

young girls, very beautiful in costumes of pure
white, and round-eyed little children, and many
barking, leaping dogs.

What a home-coming that was! Within the
heart of A-Leek-Chea-Ahoosh there burned a deep
and solemn joy because he had passed through his
first ordeal safely and was with his own people once
more. Never before had he realized how dear they
were to him, these people to whom he was bound
by traditional ties of blood and tender love. How
close they all were, they and the land they loved,
this country of mountains and plains and running
streams, the land of the Crows!

There was excitement and laughter, many ex-
planations, much glad talk. All of them saw the
scalp. One of their own, a boy of sixteen, had
scalped a Sioux alive and had returned to his village
unharmed! Surely it must be that the Great Spirit
looked kindly down upon these, His chosen children, the Crows, and made them strong of arm
and fearless of heart, since even their boys could
conquer great Sioux warriors.

While the squaws, with the help of the little
children, set up the scalp pole and built fires and
prepared food for the feast, A-Leek-Chea-Ahoosh
stole away from the confusion, ran down to the
creek to bathe in its sparkling, icy waters, and then
into his mother's tepee to dress for this, the outstanding moment of his life. For he was the man
of the hour and he knew it.

He put on the beautiful beaded moccasins his
mother had made for him. Around his neck he
placed the chest-piece of beads made from long,
polished bones. Upon wrists and ankles he fastened
bands of elk teeth, strung on thongs, that jingled
whenever he moved. His breeches were white antelope hide, fringed at the sides and adorned with
colored porcupine quills. Upon his head he ad-
justed a headdress of painted feathers. Among
those bright feathers, now, he might add one upright eagle feather, for he was a brave; he had made
coup: he had attacked an enemy and scalped him
alive.

When A-Leek-Chea-Ahoosh had attended carefully to every detail of his feast costume he took up
the tomahawk upon which his mother had labored
so many hours. She had made the handle beautiful,
polishing and carving it, and tying to it long
streamers of elk hide, beaded and fringed, that
fluttered as the boy walked.

Carrying it as a New Yorker carries his cane,
the young Indian Beau Brummell pushed back the
flap of the tepee and stepped out into view, a resplendent figure in his gala attire. His fine dark
head was proudly poised. His eyes glowed in a face
that was earnest and thoughtful. Glancing over
the assembled group his eyes met the eyes of the
old mother and read in them a fierce joy.

They had a feast in which everyone joined,
chief and headmen, squaws and young girls and

children. After that came the medicine smoke
for the braves. Pretty Eagle drew a long breath of
smoke from his red stone pipe and pressed it to
the ground and gestured with it to the east, the
west, the north, the south. Then, solemnly, he
passed it into the hand of the proud, trembling,
eager boy, who, for the first time, was taking his
man's place with the warriors of his tribe. He too
smoked and passed the pipe round until it had made
the complete circle.

Then came the parade on horseback, the warriors in gorgeous war bonnets that trailed on the
ground, squaws and girls in robes completely covered with elk teeth. Round and round the roaring
camp fire they rode in ever widening circles, giving
their war whoops, singing songs of triumph to the
beat of the drums.

And as they sang, their hearts warmed with
pride and gladness. They were patriots, loving
their land with a great love. Patriotism, tribal
loyalty, that same frenzied emotion that swells our
hearts at sight of our flag, that same fury of joy
that stirred in us when we learned that our "Lone
Eagle" had landed safe on French soil.

Doubtless the young hero A-Leek-Chea-Ahoosh
strutted a little with excusable boyish pride, as he
walked up to the scalp pole and struck it a ringing
blow with his tomahawk and chanted the story of
his adventure. We know that even today the heart
of the old chief, Plenty Coups, beats a little faster

as he sits with his friends, relating the tale of how he first made coup.

To the boy, that night seventy years ago, it seemed that the voice of the wind in the pine trees was no longer mournful. It sang a soft paean and he could fancy that it was the voice of his brother speaking to him.

"Do not grieve longer for me," the voice said. "You have avenged my death. Think no longer of snows that have fallen but of snows yet to fall. Make many coups, grow very strong and courageous, so that you will be worthy to be chief of our people. Do not grieve."

And, in the heart of A-Leek-Chea-Ahoosh, down beneath his boy's vanity and his pride, was a deep, still gladness.

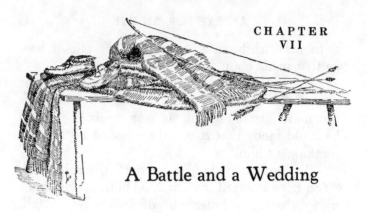

A Battle and a Wedding

A TALL, thin man, sitting his horse very erect, was riding back and forth past the hundreds of tepees that made up the village of the Mountain Crows. He wore buckskin leggins and red flannel shirt and white man's broad-brimmed hat. Beneath the hat two long braids of black hair into which strips of red flannel had been twisted hung to his shoulders. On his feet were beaded moccasins and over his shoulders a bright plaid blanket.

He was the official camp crier and, as he rode along, he chanted his message. All the people in the tepees, all the men and squaws and little children, came rushing out to hear what he had to say.

"There is to be a council meeting in the lodge of the chief," he intoned. "Tonight, in the tepee of Pretty Eagle, a council meeting."

That night there gathered around the camp fire in front of Pretty Eagle's lodge all the rising young bucks, the headmen, the warriors and sub-chiefs. It was a warm night in late fall. All about them as they sat in waiting silence smoking the medicine pipe spattered the bronzed leaves of the quaking asps, sounding like raindrops. Beyond the small golden circle of the fire was the darkness, thick, velvety, ominous.

Within that inner golden circle, taking his place among the personages of the Crow tribe— men who had distinguished themselves by some outstanding act of bravery—sat A-Leek-Chea-Ahoosh. He was a lad past twenty now, not overly tall nor exceptionally robust, but with eager, quest-ing eyes that glowed in a face that was thoughtful and strong and fine. He, like all the others, waited in patient silence till the Great Spirit should move their chief to speak. Finally the old man rose.

"You all know what has happened to us," he said. "You know that from time to time the Sioux have stolen from us, the Crows, many horses. In their last raid they stole a hundred head. And we have done nothing. Soon the enemy will say we have squaws' hearts. Our enemy have become very strong, very daring. They steal our horses, they come to our hunting ground to kill our buffalo and elk and bear. Next they will take from us our land of tall grasses and running water, our beauti-ful land of mountains and valleys, the land for which our fathers' fathers fought. Then our women and children will wander homeless, like stray dogs. They will die of hunger and cold. We will have no place to set our tepees, we, the great tribe of Crows, who for hundreds of years have held the valley of the Echeta Casha.

"Do our enemies speak with crooked tongues or have our young men the hearts of squaws that they permit this thing to be? Are there no brave warriors among you who will recover our horses and teach the Sioux that they cannot molest the Crows? I have spoken."

There were many young men that night to burn hot with shame at the scornful words of their old chief, many to spring to their feet, alert, fearless, ready to make war upon the Sioux. But first among them all was the young brave, A-Leek-Chea-Ahoosh, he whom the world was to know later as "Plenty Coups," he who as a child had outrun all of the boys of the tribe, outswum them, killed more buffalo than any of the others, who from the first desired to become "not only as good as the best, but the best," and who, though only nineteen, had already made coup.

It was of him, this young A-Leek-Chea-Ahoosh, the squaws chattered as they went out along the creek gathering bull-berries, or onto the plains to cut up the meat their men had killed.

"He will be the greatest warrior of them all," the squaws said. "His heart knows no fear, his body no weariness."

And many mothers, counseling their daughters in the seclusion of their tepees, said: "A-Leek-Chea-Ahoosh will become a mighty warrior. His woman will never need to blush with shame because her man is a coward. He is a mighty hunter. His woman will never be without meat in her tepee or robes for her dresses. He will have many horses. His woman need never walk, dragging her tepee poles, when the camp moves. He is kind to all things, children and horses and dogs. His woman need never fear his anger."

It was toward A-Leek-Chea-Ahoosh the shy bright eyes of the maidens turned most often as they sat whispering and laughing while they polished bone beads for their feast costumes. Whenever he approached they covered their faces modestly with their shawls, but not before daring young eyes had given him gay glances of welcome. It was upon him they smiled most often as they danced at the wedding and birthday feasts.

Now, at the words of Chief Pretty Eagle, the young man sprang to his feet. There was a gallant poise of the head, a glow of the steady eyes, a firmness of the lips that ever won for him the trust and respect of the old men.

"Our chief has spoken," he said. "It is well that we show the Sioux we have not squaw hearts. I have seen the trail of the enemy. I know that it leads toward the rising sun, into the valley of the Big Horn. I will follow that trail and I will fight the enemy and recapture our stolen horses. I will be so strong, so brave, that ever after the Sioux shall fear the Crows."

"A-Leek-Chea-Ahoosh has spoken wise words," Pretty Eagle said, gravely. "He shall lead twenty of our braves. The squaws shall fill the parfleche boxes. The small boys shall get in the horses. He will travel many sleeps. He will take many arrows, for the enemy is strong. After one sleep and one sun he will start and follow the dark trail toward the rising sun, toward the valley of the Big Horn."

So, very early next morning the entire village was awake and stirring. All the women and children worked excitedly. The squaws, some of them mothers of the lads who were going out on their first warpath, prepared buffalo meat and pemmican and filled the parfleche boxes, those rawhide boxes with lids which were to be strapped to the horses' sides.

And the boys, those still too young for the warpath, went out onto the plains, envy and admiration for their older brothers burning in their hearts, and rounded up and drove into camp the fleetest horses.

At length, when everything was in readiness, A-Leek-Chea-Ahoosh and the twenty braves, with their quivers of arrows and their knives and war clubs and coup sticks, their parfleche boxes of meat and their war regalia, mounted their horses and rode away across the dusk-tinted plains, heading south and east toward the Big Horn Mountains.

And many old mothers, hearts torn with pride

Big Horn Cañon. Here A-Leek-Chea-Ahoosh led his braves in battle against the Sioux and made coup. Photograph by Allen. See page 135.

and grief, stood, hands shading their eyes, to watch the young riders galloping swiftly over the silent plains until they were but a speck against the horizon and then were swallowed up in twilight shadows. And they prayed mutely to the Great Spirit that He guard their sons and bring them safe home. And many young girls prayed, silently, as they watched.

A-Leek-Chea-Ahoosh rode along and his heart sang. The sun dipped down back of the mountains and the stars came out and the vast, lonely, still plain sparkled silver-white with moonlight.

There welled up within him a deep love for this land of his, the land for which the people of his tribe had fought and suffered, the land for which many had died as his brother had died. Miles of sagebrush and cactus and greasewood; miles of waving buffalo grass, frosted now, rustling crisply; buttes and hills and coulees and rivers and plains; cottonwood trees and quaking asps and willows and pines. The majesty of wide-spread, still distances, the majesty of the Blue, hovering very close, the majesty of the mountains so much a part of his youth, so vital a background to his entire life that he could not conceive an existence apart from them. There was anguish and joy in the mute worship he gave them. Each—or so it seemed to him then, in his youthful, forward leaping arrogance, the mountains and himself—was intertwined with the other. Neither could exist separately.

Years later, when many snows had fallen upon the proud dark head of A-Leek-Chea-Ahoosh, when he felt the time had come for his body to go back to Mother Earth and his soul to the Great Spirit Chief, he spoke before an assembly of red men and whites. He told them of his deep and abiding love for his country, the land of his fathers, made sacred by the graves of the departed.

"I want you people," he said, "of the great plains country beyond the mighty waters of the Mississippi to come and visit the scenes of my boyhood where then the red man was lord and now the white man rules."

But the boy riding gayly over unfenced plains on his first raid against the enemy, was young and strong and carefree. Nor could he then, by any stretch of imagination, foresee a time when red men might cease to be lords of the land they loved.

And so the boy's heart sang, frosty night air nipped his flesh pleasantly, he tingled to his very finger tips with excitement. This was his first adventure as leader of men. Another long stride, if he proved wise and brave, toward the distant goal he had set himself—chief of his tribe.

He began to sing softly a song his mother had sung to him on cozy winter nights in their tepee when he was a little lad, just as he was dropping off to sleep:

Every day go out to fight the enemy,
Every day be very strong and brave.
Be fleet of foot,
And sure with bow and arrow.
Always make the enemy run.

With the help of his medicine he would, on this raid, be very brave; he would make the enemy run.

Chancing to glance up he saw high in the Blue just over his head a great eagle with wide-spread wings. Then the heart of the boy leaped within him for the eagle was his strong medicine. It had come to him now when he needed courage, and so nothing could harm him; no Sioux arrow could hit him.

A-Leek-Chea-Ahoosh thought happy thoughts as his pony jogged along over the silver-sprinkled plains. There would be feasting and dancing when he and his band of braves returned. All the wise old men and the medicine men and the chiefs would say: "A-Leek-Chea-Ahoosh is a man. He is a brave man. He is going to be a great warrior."

The young hunter, Bell Rock, might be there to see A-Leek-Chea-Ahoosh riding triumphantly into the Crow village, with enemy scalps and all the stolen horses. More than any other A-Leek-Chea-Ahoosh desired that his friend Bell Rock should witness the victorious homecoming. There was much talk of Bell Rock as chief of the River

Crows. He had brought in the scalp of an enemy as well as an enemy's picketed horse, and therefore had made coups twice while A-Leek-Chea-Ahoosh had as yet captured no picketed horse and had struck coup but once. A friendly rivalry existed between the two young men.

Whenever he thought of his friend Bell Rock the heart of A-Leek-Chea-Ahoosh was warm, for he liked the young River Crow and admired his strength and courage. Nevertheless he burned with the ambition to excel him in all undertakings.

A-Leek-Chea-Ahoosh foresaw the time, not far distant, when the Mountain and the River Crows would be united with one great chief ruling all the Crow people. At the thought his pulses pounded. He determined, with the help of the Great Spirit and his strong medicine, to become that chief.

Much depended upon the result of this raid upon the Sioux. Today he must prove himself an able leader of men, a brave warrior, tireless, strong, fearless, alert.

The maidens would smile upon him the night he danced around the scalp pole and recounted his battle with the Sioux. And the one maiden who was the most beautiful of all the Crow maidens, the most beautiful in the world, would be there. A-Leek-Chea-Ahoosh had given her a name which he never spoke aloud—"Flying Bird"—because he thought her small feet, in their soft beaded moccasins, beneath the fringe of her elk-hide robe, were like little flying birds when she danced.

And he fancied that her eyes, when for a fleeting second they looked into his, said something mysterious and beautiful that made his heart sing with joy. Often they said something that was like the soft music of the voices of the night wind, which one could not understand, could scarcely hear, could only feel.

Flying Bird would be sure to be waiting, smiling, as he rode triumphantly into camp, driving ahead of him the long string of horses.

It was a journey of two sleeps from the village of the Crows to the hunting camp of the Sioux on the Big Horn. The young Crows traveled the dark trail, resting daytimes under cottonwood trees down in coulees where they would be hidden from enemy wolves on lookout peaks.

They came to a country that was rough, with high rimrocks encircling a valley gashed by dry runs and coulees. Here there were countless places behind buttes or in cañons or cottonwood groves where the enemy might hide, even with their large band of horses. Often A-Leek-Chea-Ahoosh motioned his men to halt and got down to put his ear to the ground, but as yet the earth gave no sound. There was no pulse of horses' feet.

Constantly his sharp eyes studied the stony trail, searching for marks of the enemy. And he came at last to the Little Horn where the crumbled bank showed that many horses had crossed. The moon was shining straight down into the valley. He crept along a little way on foot, leading his horse and studying the trail. Presently he noticed that some of the stones on the river bank were scratched.

"White man's horses," he said, and he pointed to the scratched stones. "Fresh tracks, heading toward the Big Horn. Before another sleep we catch them."

Ever more distinct, more easily followed, grew the tracks of the Sioux. They, it appeared, considered themselves safe and were making no effort to cover their trail. No longer did A-Leek-Chea-Ahoosh sing aloud. He and his braves must advance cautiously, sending scouts ahead. But his blood was hot with the thrill of the chase and his heart sang. "Every day go out to fight the enemy. Every day be very strong and brave."

Finally, ear to the ground, he felt the rhythmic throb of the beat of horses' feet. Quickly he pulled up over him the skin of a wolf—a necessary part of an Indian raider's equipment—covering his arms, his legs, even his head, so that from a distance he could not be told from a wolf. And he climbed to the top of a high butte and prowled about on all fours and sent the weird wolf-howl far out across the valley. For a distance of many miles his sharp eyes studied the country and could see no life save that of grazing buffalo along the river bank and a band of sheep up on a stony crag of a mountain. At length, after a patient hour, he thought he detected, down in the shadows of a broad, shallow cañon miles away, a splotch darker than the massed darkness of the pines. Intently he watched that splotch and he saw that it moved and spread out and closed together again. Presently he saw a faint curl of smoke. That must be the camp of the thieving Sioux with their large band of horses, so confident in their covert that they dare build a fire.

Cautiously, on all fours, A-Leek-Chea-Ahoosh slid down the butte and back to his waiting braves. From now on every move must be governed by prudence and cunning, for doubtless there were enemy wolves prowling about on lookout peaks, spying upon the Crows, just as the Crows were spying upon the Sioux.

"I have seen the enemy," the young leader announced, "and they are many. Because of their drove of stolen horses they cannot travel fast. We will fight them, even though they are many and we are few, for we are Crow warriors, so brave that all tribes fear us. We will take from the Sioux our horses which they have stolen, and the white man's horses with shoes, and all the horses of the Sioux. We will make coup and return to our people with many horses and scalps.

"Ten of you, with Big Shoulders, will circle these hills from behind, where you cannot be seen, and will come upon the enemy from the other way, through that narrow pass. The rest of us will attack at the wide mouth of the cañon. We will shoot our arrows and give our war cry. They will see that they are surrounded and they will think that we are many—as the blades of grass on the plains. We must move quickly, before they go on through that pass and join their people at the Sioux village, or else, against all of them, we will be like a puff of dust in the wind, and tonight our scalps will hang from the Sioux scalp poles."

So Big Shoulders, with ten men, circled the hills. Meanwhile A-Leek-Chea-Ahoosh, with ten others, approached the wide mouth of the cañon, not in company formation, riding abreast, for that would be foolhardy; but advancing cautiously, scattered over a wide space, so that the Sioux, even though they saw one of the riders, or two, should not suspect an organized attack.

They rode along slowly, like hunters searching for the trail of buffalo, yet as quietly as they could through the knee-deep carpet of dry, crackling leaves that seemed with every step to cry out a warning to the Sioux.

No one seeing them jogging along with such apparent unconcern could have guessed that the young Crow braves had knowledge of the proximity of an enemy, or any fear of the danger of a poisoned arrow that might come whining from behind butte or boulder to end their lives.

Proudly, at the head of the straggling band of

horsemen, rode A-Leek-Chea-Ahoosh, for it was the leader who must always take the brunt of the danger, inspire his men with courage, and be the first to fall. He was jubilant. He felt no fear.

He was within a few yards of the yawning mouth of the cañon. Now that he was on its level he could not see far in, for it went twisting up between two high hills. But, from its cool dark depths he could hear the trickle of a mountain stream and the click of horses' feet on stones and the voices of the Sioux.

Turning to his men he gave a sign and they gathered quickly around him. They could tell by the sound that the enemy were coming nearer and ever nearer the mouth of the ravine. They waited in silence until the big band of horses came plunging and snorting out into the open. Behind the horses, around a bend, came the Sioux warriors, twenty-five or thirty of them, grim, hard-visaged, unsmiling men, chanting their war song as they rode along. And now the Sioux leader saw the little group of waiting Crows. He was quick with his bow and arrow, but not quick enough. There came a thin whine. That was the arrow of A-Leek-Chea-Ahoosh as it went singing its way straight to the heart of the enemy. The Sioux threw up his hands and tumbled off his horse, face downward, among the scrub pines of the coulee.

Then the Crows yelled their war cry and charged into the cañon, right into the face of the astonished Sioux braves, driving them back and back, whence they had come. And now, all at once, the air was full of yells and whining arrows. The coulee was full of a chaotic mass of panting, sweating, writhing bodies, the bodies of horses and men, of Sioux and Crow. And arrows came whizzing from the ambush of dead horses, from rocks, trees, from any and every hiding-place behind which men could cower.

A Sioux dropped off his horse and lay silent, motionless, and his frightened horse went plunging down the steep, rocky coulee. Another Sioux fell, and another. Brave men though they were, and valiant warriors, they were utterly bewildered by this unexpected attack. Scurrying to shelter—here —there—anywhere—the deadly arrows of the Crows stopped them midway.

Slowly, fighting desperately under rain of Crow arrows, the remaining Sioux abandoned their horses and inched their way back up the coulee. The high narrow pass was their only hope of escape. But now, behind them, sounded the war cry of the Crows. Through the opening came leaping the little company under Big Shoulders, seeming to the terrified Sioux as many as the stars in the Blue. They were surrounded. Their last chance of retreat was cut off.

And now arrows were cast aside. They fought, Crows and Sioux, hand to hand, with war clubs and knives. The Sioux were not outnumbered but they thought they were and the thought weakened their resistance. They continued to fight, but desperately, without hope.

The deep, dark, cool cañon, moss-carpeted, dripping with vines, where the Sioux had watered their horses and roasted buffalo meat at camp fires but a moment since, still, save for the swish of pines and the tinkle of the little stream, was now hideous with the clamor of stampeded horses, rearing and snorting, trampling wounded men underfoot as they plunged out into the open. It echoed to the cry of the victorious Crows and the moan of dying Sioux. It was raucous with the heavy rasping breathing of wary men, circling, dodging each other, hatred in their eyes, waiting their chance to strike.

And the stream went dancing merrily on its way, carrying with it crimson blotches of blood— Sioux blood—the blood of men who had for so long made war upon the Crows, stealing from them their horses, their buffalo, and their women.

Young A-Leek-Chea-Ahoosh seemed to be everywhere at once. The Great Spirit was kind to him, his strong medicine very strong indeed. He leaped safely away from the flying hoofs of a horse maddened with fear. He dodged an arrow coming from behind a rock that missed him by a hair's breadth. He jumped onto a rock and, with his war club, crushed in the head of a Sioux brave crouching there. A dull thud, a moan, and one more of the enemy crumpled down, a sprawling thing no longer to be feared.

Four Sioux, the last remaining alive, had managed to skulk back into a small cave in the side of the coulee and were huddled there, sending arrows down. At their feet lay one of their own men with a Crow arrow through his heart. A-Leek-Chea-Ahoosh saw those Sioux entrenched in their dugout. He saw the dead brave at their feet. He gave a yell. He went leaping from rock to rock between the rain of arrows, up to the very mouth of the cave, and there, where all could see, both Sioux and Crows, while arrows came whining down about him he struck the dead Sioux with his war club, and then sprang back behind a boulder beyond harm's way.

He had made coup. He had made the greatest coup of all, for he had in the midst of enemy arrows struck one of the fallen. Such an act, in the ethics of Indian warfare, requires the highest form of courage.

Presently, of all the Sioux who had expected to reach home that night with their stolen horses, not one was left alive.

The Crow braves had won. They were mighty warriors. And now they could pause to rest and survey the scene of battle. A-Leek-Chea-Ahoosh felt no weariness. He was exalted. His pulses were pounding with a frenzied joy. At last he had caught up with that ambitious friend of his, Bell

Rock, and now the race for the chieftainship would be a neck-to-neck race. Each had made two coups. Bell Rock had brought in an enemy's scalp and an enemy's picketed horse; but A-Leek-Chea-Ahoosh had scalped a Sioux alive and he had struck a dead Sioux in the very midst of the enemies' rain of arrows.

He was exultant. He was, all at once, very anxious to have ended the long journey back across the valley of the Big Horn and to be at home. Vain, as arrogant youth is always vain, he anticipated the triumphant entry he would make into the Crow village, driving ahead of him all the horses, leading his twenty men, not one of them wounded.

The old men would say: "A-Leek-Chea-Ahoosh is strong and fearless. Though his heart is young yet his head is wise and old. He knows how to lead men into battle. Before many snows he will be one of our headmen."

And Flying Bird, the little girl with the dancing feet and the shining eyes, would say nothing with her lips. But her eyes—those eyes that often spoke strange, beautiful, wordless messages straight from her heart to the heart of A-Leek-Chea-Ahoosh—they would say: "I am proud of you."

A-Leek-Chea-Ahoosh called together his men. Hurriedly they carried the bodies of the fallen foe into a cottonwood grove at the head of the cañon and laid them there to sleep their last sleep. Beside them the Crows placed bows and arrows, and bits of meat from parfleche boxes, to aid them on their perilous journey across the Slippery Log to the Spirit Land. And over all the Crows piled rocks, completely covering the dead.

They had been brave, those defeated Sioux. They had fought gallantly to the last. And an Indian always respects the courage of another, even though that other be an enemy.

Then the Crows went out onto the plains and rounded up the horses and began their homeward journey. They must travel slowly now; for twenty men to drive over a hundred half-wild horses across a country gashed with coulees and dry runs is no easy matter.

All the way the heart of A-Leek-Chea-Ahoosh sang. He was burning with impatience. He wished that he might speed on, night and day, without pause for food or water or rest. He wished for the wings of a bird, the strong wings of the eagle, to bear him swiftly back to camp so that his eyes might at once look into the eyes of the girl Flying Bird and read her heart's message.

The first gray light of dawn was over everything. Little mountain birds were twittering sleepily. The air out on the plains was sweet and stingingly cool. The boy drew a long breath and glanced up into the sky. And there, directly over his head, far up in the Blue, soared an eagle, with

wide, strong outspread wings. His strong medicine! He knew then that all would be well with
him.

That morning the Crow village was early astir.
There had been long anxious hours of waiting after
the young warriors had ridden away to battle
against the Sioux. But just now a runner had come
dashing with the news that from his lookout peak
he had seen the victors returning. Soon they would
be here with many horses, more than he could
count. Fires were built, food prepared, for the
braves would be tired and hungry. And then
everyone, from Pretty Eagle himself and the head
men and the medicine men down to the little children and the dogs, went far out onto the plains to
welcome their braves. Old squaws went out, their
mother-hearts warm with gladness that their sons
were safe home again. Fathers, old men, too feeble
for the hunt or the battle, filled with pride at the
valor of the young ones.

And they all saw the big band of driven horses
and the dangling scalps, and the Crow warriors,
riding their horses proudly, not one of them
wounded.

And among the young girls who came running
out was one who looked first at A-Leek-Chea-
Ahoosh, and saw him sitting erect and strong and
fearless, leading his band of braves, a smile upon his
lips, a flash of gladness in his eyes. It seemed to her
that he was searching eagerly for someone. She
advanced, timidly, a step beyond the others. And

then, amidst all the clamor, the shouts of triumph, the chattering, the laughter, the barking of dogs and the whinnying of tired horses glad to be home once more, their eyes met, the eyes of Flying Bird and A-Leek-Chea-Ahoosh, and spoke, silently, joyfully.

His eyes said, plainly: "I wish to take you for my woman. I will take you to my tepee to be my woman forever."

And she smiled and drew her blanket quickly over her face, but not before her eyes had answered his: "I will be glad to go to your tepee with you, for you are the strongest and bravest of all the young men of the Crows."

There was hustle and bustle in the Crow camp that day. While the braves rested and while the old men sat around the fire, smoking and talking wise talk, the squaws prepared for the sun dance they would have in the evening. They set up the scalp pole and hung on it the Sioux scalps their sons had taken. They roasted quantities of the boss ribs of buffalo and tender, fat buffalo tongue. Then there was pemmican, and sweet cakes made of wild honey. The girls helped too, though their minds were busy with thoughts of the fringed and beaded robes they would wear that night.

At last the sun sank behind the mountains and the Old Woman shone up in the Blue, and the feast began, and the smoking and dancing. Presently one of the warriors sprang forward and struck the

Doctor Allen in the days when he and the West were young. See page 150.

scalp pole a ringing blow with his coup stick. And
then, to the low rhythmic beat of the tom-toms,
and to the soft crooning accompaniment of the
squaws, he danced round the pole and chanted a
recital of his adventures. He told of the courage
and wisdom and strength of the Crows and of the
cruel cunning of their foes, the Sioux.

Another warrior joined him, and another, and,
last of all, A-Leek-Chea-Ahoosh. He struck the
scalp pole. He danced. His feet caught the gliding
movement. Every graceful, intricate step told,
more eloquently than words, of the thing he had
done and of the things he hoped to do. His young
slim strong body swayed and bent like a sapling in
the breeze. The dull monotonous insistent, mes-
meric rhythm of the tom-tom flowed over him,
sank deep down into him, until he became intoxicated by its power.

He ceased to be a man. He felt himself a young
god, fearless, strong, aching to do impossible deeds
of valor for his tribe and his land and for the
woman he loved. A stabbing rapture welled up
within him, and his dancing feet flew faster and
faster. His comrades dropped out of the dancing
circle exhausted, and others took their places, but
A-Leek-Chea-Ahoosh danced on and on. A young
god cannot tire. His body was aflame with the two
emotions strongest in the breast of man—love of
country and love of woman. He was a Crow.
These were his people to whom he was bound by

a thousand ties of blood and association. This was
his country, this beautiful land, and the Crows
were unconquerable and would keep it forever,
against the Sioux, against the Blackfeet, against
the Pawnees, against all enemies.

And the girl sitting over there among the
squaws, swaying, smiling, watching him with shining eyes, was to be his woman.

All these thoughts for which the boy had no
words he expressed in his jubilant dance which lasted through the night, until the squaws nodded with
sleep and the camp fire burned down, until the sun
crept up over the eastern mountains.

Then A-Leek-Chea-Ahoosh ran out onto the
plains and gazed about him at the radiant glory of
river and mountain and frosted valley. He stood
alone. He was drunk with love and youth. He felt
himself ageless with the eternal youth of the mountains.

Noiselessly, while all the people slept, he
rounded up twenty of his horses, leaving only one
for himself, and led them to the tepee where Flying
Bird lived with her mother. He tied the horses
there. When they wakened they would find them.
Then, if the mother deemed the gift worthy of her
daughter, she would keep the horses and give the
girl to A-Leek-Chea-Ahoosh to be his woman.

He went back to his own tepee and dropped
down on his soft bed of robes and fell asleep. He
slept until the sun was high in the Blue and until
all the noises of the village wakened him. For a

moment, in that state of hovering bliss between waking and sleeping, he lay, endeavoring to collect his thoughts. He yawned and stretched and grinned, more happy animal than thoughtful man. Then suddenly he remembered. He sprang to his feet and pulled aside the curtain of his tepee and looked across to the tepee where Flying Bird lived with her mother. His horses were not picketed there. The old mother had led them away. She had accepted his gift.

The boy turned and gazed up at the mountains as he always did in moments of deep grief or swelling joy. They had shared every passion of his young life. They were the temple at which he worshipped his diety. Now his heart was beating fast with rapture.

He ran down to the creek to bathe and back to his tepee to dress. He put on new elk-hide leggins, fringed down the sides, and his best beaded moccasins, and the exquisitely beaded belt his mother had made for his last birthday gift. He wished to appear resplendent in the eyes of Flying Bird. Then he went in and out among all the tepees, searching for her but telling no one for whom he was searching. And finally he found her standing alone down by the creek, hidden by a clump of chokecherry bushes.

Though she saw him coming she did not cover her face with her blanket. She stood, straight and calm and beautiful, waiting proudly for her lover. He put his arm around her and felt the trembling of her slim body and the fast beating of her heart against his own, like the heart of a little captured frightened bird.

He whispered: "Will your lips speak to me as your eyes for long have spoken? Will you be my woman?"

The eyes she raised to his were tender and solemn. "I will be your woman," she told him. "I love you. I trust you. I know that you will be kind to me. But whether you were kind or not, I would still love you and serve you forever."

That night, once more, there was feasting and dancing in the Crow village, a betrothal feast this time. There was much laughter and many good-natured jokes. A-Leek-Chea-Ahoosh and his bride laughed and danced, though sometimes they were made to blush at the jokes.

But when the gayety was at its height, when everyone was too excited to notice, the boy put his arm around the waist of Flying Bird and led her away from all the noisy hilarity into the dark stillness of the trees where his tepee stood.

He was her man now, and she was his woman.

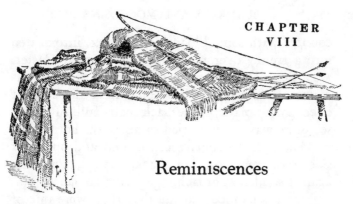

Reminiscences

TWILIGHT on the plains of Montana Territory, its stillness shattered by the rumbling and lurching and creaking of a long wagon train that was winding its slow way between buttes and over cactus and sagebrush. Fifty-six wagons, heavily loaded, four horses to a wagon, and, for each wagon, two men, the driver and the bull-whacker. Again and again the sharp crack of long whips rang out into the silence like pistol shots. The horses crunched along over thick frost-crisped buffalo grass, heads drooping, stumbling from weariness.

The outfit had been traveling all day through blazing heat, and they were tired—men and horses—and hungry and thirsty. They were making their way to the banks of Little Big Horn where they hoped, without too great risk from Indians, to picket horses, build fires, and cook buffalo meat and coffee.

They had come from Wyoming Territory. Miles back, early in the day, at a spot where Dayton, Wyoming, now stands, they had had an en-

counter with some bloodthirsty Sioux, intoxicated
into a frenzy over their recent victory at Custer.
Any doubts concerning the success of that en-
counter Old Grizzly Bill could have dispelled at
once by displaying the sack half full of Sioux
scalps he was carrying tied to his saddle horn.

Ahead of the outfit and behind and on either
side rode men on horseback, armed, guarding
against sudden approach of warring Indians.

Far in advance—so far that they were out of
sight and hearing of the wagons—rode Old Grizzly
Bill and a young man from Ohio who had that day,
following the skirmish with the Sioux, been appointed leader of the expedition. He was known
throughout the New West as "Doc Bill Allen,"
blacksmith by trade, hunter, trapper, scout, by
choice, athirst always for adventure and more adventure.

The two men jogged along without speech,
keeping a vigilant lookout for Indians on the warpath. They knew they were in the Crow Reservation now, and that any moment a whizzing arrow
from behind butte or boulder might voice resent-
ment of their intrusion. And presently they saw
what they were looking for and did not desire to
see: a party of Indian braves riding rapidly through
the golden dusk from Pryor Creek way. Two
white men on tired horses against some twenty Indians, a scant half mile between them and the
Indians, three or four miles between them and
their outfit.

Gripping guns they wheeled to make the dash back to the protection of the wagons. But the Indians had seen them. They came plunging on, guns pointed, through thick clouds of dust.

"We'll never make it," Doc muttered, between set teeth. "Might as well wait and take what's coming to us."

"They'll never—never get me alive," Old Grizzly panted, and he pressed his gun to his side.

But Allen yelled out a sharp "Stop! Don't be a fool!"

The Indians were within speaking distance. They had paused and were sitting their horses, guns ready, eyeing the two white men with glowering suspicion. And it was then Allen noticed what dispelled something of the fear chilling his blood— saw that the hair of the red men was roached. That meant they were Crows, and Crows had always been friendly to white men. At once Allen spurred his horse forward until he was face to face with the Indian leader, a young man, slender, strong, with a fearless stern countenance and sharp watchful eyes. Those eyes were demanding of Allen his business on Crow land.

Promptly Allen gave the sign of the Crow, but the grim face of the young Indian did not soften. Those were strenuous days, fraught with danger, when it behooved all men to be on their guard, wary, distrustful, until a friendship was proved.

"How!" said Allen.

The Indian sat motionless, silent, lips tight.

Just then, from across dusk-shadowed plains could be heard the distinct rumble of wagons and voices of men and crack of whips. And now, circling the foot of hills, they were winding into view. Sharp with distrust the eyes of the Crow brave questioned Allen.

"Tell him," Allen said to Old Grizzly, "tell him we're not going to make trouble. We're not going to hunt buffalo. Tell him we're on our way up into the mountains after gold. Tell him we'd like to camp this one night on their land."

With grave unbelieving courtesy the Indian listened to the words of the interpreter. He bowed his acknowledgment but made no further reply. He must have added proof that these whites were friends of the Crows and not allies of the Blackfeet or the Sioux. Often palefaces spoke with crooked tongues.

Allen assured him in sign language: "We are friends of your people. We do not wish to war upon Crows. In our wagons we have much buffalo meat. Elk meat. We will build a fire. We will have a feast. We will share with our friends, the Crows."

The young brave did not move, did not speak, sat his horse in haughty silence, watching the approach of the jolting wagons. Though he and his twenty warriors were now outnumbered ten to one, he made no effort toward flight nor friendly gesture of propitiation, merely sat in calm silence viewing the hustle and bustle attendant upon the making of camp.

The wagons were driven in a circle, wheels interlocking, forming within a well-nigh unbreakable stockade. One small opening was left through which horses could be driven at night. Then the tired animals were unhitched and turned out to graze with two scouts guarding them, lest they be stampeded by bears or wolves or Indians.

Meanwhile men were dragging in dried branches of cottonwood and building a fire and setting over it big pots of coffee. Other men took out from the wagons chunks of buffalo meat and venison and that choicest of all delicacies, fat buffalo tongues.

Soon the smell of wood smoke and of sizzling meat and boiling coffee began to fill the air and that tantalizing smell accomplished what all Allen's vows of friendship had failed to do: dispelled the grim suspicion from the faces of the Crows. They sniffed, they exchanged glances, they smiled, and then with one accord they leaped from their horses and came toward the fire.

Without a word, emulating their own silence, Allen took from glowing ashes a big hunk of meat, dripping with fat, and proffered it on its stick to the young Indian headman. Gravely he accepted and divided it, giving to each of his men a portion. They ate ravenously, as though they had been a long time without food.

They ventured still nearer the fire and joined the whites, sitting cross-legged on the ground. The silence had become suddenly less strained, less ominous. They were given all they could eat of roast buffalo and venison, and later, appetites somewhat appeased, bits of fat buffalo tongue. Coffee was poured for them, and Allen, who knew the weakness of these red men of the plains, made it into a thick syrup with sugar. They sipped the hot nectar and smacked their lips, smiling, and drank with big gulps of appreciation. The flashing eyes of the young Crow leader warmed into a rather reluctant friendliness. In spite of himself his wall of reserve was being battered down by Doc Allen's persistent hospitality.

After the long ceremonious feast was over and the men, whites and reds, sprawled in companionable comfort around the fire smoking pipes, the Crows sought news of the outside world. The whites told of the battle between Custer's men and the Sioux, which the Crows, of course, already knew.

"We took part in that battle," the young brave reminded them with fine pride. "We, the Crows, fought with the whites against the Sioux. We have given our friendship to our white brothers and hope for a lasting peace."

The Indians listened with intense interest to Allen's account of the skirmish he and his men had had that day with the Sioux. To verify the story Old Grizzly Bill displayed his sack of Sioux scalps and in a burst of rare generosity gave one to the Crow leader.

The warrior smiled his gratitude for the gift. "The Sioux are our enemies," he said. "They have always taken our horses and killed our buffalo. Since the Custer battle they have many white man's guns. Bullets. We, the Crows, have few guns. Pretty bad."

In reply Allen gave him five needle guns taken from the Sioux that day. He said: "Our White Father in Washington is having a fort built at Custer, to be called 'Fort Custer,' which will protect the Crows from their enemies, the Sioux, and make the whole country safe both for the Crows and their brothers, the whites."

The Indian bowed his understanding of the words. He was favorably impressed by the hospitality and the generosity of these his white brothers.

Allen went on: "The Sioux have broken treaties with the whites; so have the Cheyennes and Pawnees and Blackfeet. But our White Father in Washington knows the Crows have always kept their faith."

For a moment, in silence, the Crow brave gazed thoughtfully into the fire. Then his straightforward glance met Allen's. "Since we made the first treaty with our White Father," he said, proudly, "we, the Crows, have never killed a white man. It is our wish that the whites and the Crows be friendly forever."

He rose and, stepping over the bodies of the men sprawled all about the fire, reached Allen's side. Gravely he extended his hand.

"May your moccasins," he said, "make many tracks in the snow."

Gladly Allen gripped the proffered hand. "We are on your side," he declared, earnestly. "If enemies molest you we fight with you."

Then the young Crow placed a hand on Allen's shoulder. They were both tall men. Their eyes were on a level. "You mean that? You speak not with crooked tongue?"

"Yes," said Allen. "My heart has spoken."

The Indian pulled his knife from its sheath at his belt and extended it. The shining blade caught the red glow from the camp fire. Allen understood the significance of the act. To swear by the knife is, for an Indian, to pledge one's honor and faith, to pronounce the most sacred and lasting of vows, a vow of friendship till death.

He placed his hand on the knife. With the blackness of prairie night behind them, with the flickering flames of the camp fire lighting their faces, the two young men stood a little apart from the rest.

Allen said, slowly, "While snows continue to fall upon my head I will be your brother. My heart speaks to your heart."

And that was the beginning of the long years of friendship between Doc Bill Allen and the young brave, A-Leek-Chea-Ahoosh, to be known later throughout the world as Plenty Coups, chief of all the tribes of the Northwest.

Allen says of him that he seemed then, in spite of his youth, a "man of iron," with a cold reserve that was almost impregnable. He bore himself with an innate hauteur, his head nobly poised, his face strong and frank and fine, his eyes flashing with that pride of youth that has achieved. There was something about him that inspired confidence. He bore the mark, even then, of the born leader of men. Coming years were to teach Allen that beneath the iron reserve was a simple faith in the inherent good of men, a touching gratitude for kindness shown, a warm eagerness to be of service to those he loved.

Before the trails of the two men crossed again three years passed. During those three years, adventurous as all years in the New West must be, the young Crow brave, A-Leek-Chea-Ahoosh, had been forging steadily forward. All his youthful enthusiams, his heady ambitions, his restlessness that had been sending him out on raids against Blackfeet and Sioux, courting danger, loving it, had become centered at last in one definite urge. Far up the trail, still a giant's mighty stride away, his vague hopes and ephemeral dreams were resolving themselves into one daring desire: to prove himself worthy so that he might be made chief of his tribe. Life held for him no higher trust nor

greater glory. He loved his people, he was proud
of his heritage of Crow blood. But above and beyond all that was the inbred impulse to lead and to
govern which etches some few men of each century
and each race against the herd.

So A-Leek-Chea-Ahoosh was seizing every opportunity to test his strength, his valor and his
wisdom. He must prove himself the ablest of all
the ambitious young men of the Crows—not a
child's task that—among youth trained from baby-
hood up to worship the god of courage and
strength, who in their cradles had been lulled to
sleep with war songs, and who were quite as desirous of the chieftainship as was A-Leek-Chea-
Ahoosh himself. There was Two-Leggins, for example, a formidable rival, and his friend Bell Rock,
outstanding warrior of the River Crows, who was
running a friendly neck-to-neck race with him.

In order to become chief of his tribe an Indian
boy must make many coups. "Coup" is a word
borrowed from the French, meaning originally "a
sudden stroke," "an unexpected strategy." The
Indians, however, have restricted the use of the
word according to their own standards of valor. A
"coup" to them comprises any one of many acts:
taking an enemy's guns; taking an enemy's
picketed horse; leading a war party successfully
against an enemy; scalping an enemy; striking a
fallen foe in the thick of battle; killing an enemy
without injury to oneself. Thus two men might

make coup over one fallen foe, the one by killing
him, the other by striking him with war club under
shower of enemy arrows or bullets. At the time
when almost all tribes were living in a state of
declared war against every other tribe, to take
horses was not considered theft. The looting of
picketed horses involved the highest form of courage and skill, for it necessitated escaping vigilant
eyes of wolves on lookout points and venturing
alone into the very heart of the enemy's fortified
camp.

So, for A-Leek-Chea-Ahoosh the playtime of
youth was past. The three years since he had met
Doc Bill Allen and been his guest at the buffalo feast
in the valley of the Little Big Horn had been for
him far from idle years. During that time he had
led many war parties, some attended by success, a
few by failure. He had endured hardships, faced
dangers, and had climbed upward, step by slow
step, until he had attained an important position as
subchief under Pretty Eagle. Already he was referred to now and then as "the man who made
many coups."

Nor had time stood still for the young adven-
turer, Doc Bill Allen. Hunter, trapper, blacksmith, dentist, sharpshooter, scout, he, too, in that
young land of brave men was becoming distinguished as tireless, resourceful, fearless. Failing to
locate the rumored veins of gold up in the Big Horn
Cañon he did many things and eventually was appointed government blacksmith at Fort Custer.

Hearing footsteps approaching as he was busy at his anvil one day he glanced up to see a group of Indians standing in his doorway. He said, "How!" and went on with his work. They said, "How!" and stood watching sparks fly from the white-hot horseshoe he was shaping.

Plunging the iron into a pail of cold water presently, he stood back away from the clouds of hissing steam and discovered the Indians still standing in the doorway, waiting his pleasure in silent patience. He knew them by their roached hair to be Crows.

Having gained his attention they informed him in sign language that they wished some "bah chippay" (root-diggers) made for their squaws, and they explained very explicitly just how the tools were to be fashioned. Concluding the business on hand they turned to leave, all but one young man who lingered, smiling, at the door. From the first his fine frank friendly face had been tugging at Allen's memory.

Left alone the Crow advanced, hand extended. "We met on Little Big Horn," he reminded Doc. "Three snows ago. Much buffalo meat. Many buffalo tongues. Much sugar."

Allen laughed. "Oh, yes!" he said, "I remember now. You and I started out trying to shoot each other and ended with vows of eternal friendship."

The face of the young Crow was grave. "I meet many people. Palefaces—red men. Many talk twice. You talk once. You strong medicine."

Chief Plenty Coups and White Eagle, (Dr. Allen). Photograph by Judge Goddard. See page 156.

"Strong medicine," in the Indian's vocabulary, is an elastic and adaptable term. As A-Leek-Chea-Ahoosh used the expression it meant: "You are sincere. I trust you. Your friendship will be lasting." There was warm liking and cordial trust in the Crow's flashing eyes as he gazed into his white brother's face. That first impression Allen had received of charm and outstanding personality was strengthened in this, their second meeting. As they stood, hands clasped, the red man and the white, so similar in taste and disposition, differing in little save the color of their skin, Allen felt within him a warm admiration for this haughty young savage of the plains. He was glad that the Indian had deemed him worthy of the rare gift of friendship.

After that their trails crossed often. Doctor Allen remembers that shortly A-Leek-Chea-Ahoosh returned, bringing with him an Indian lad of about twelve, of whom he seemed very fond.

"Your son?" Allen inquired.

The Crow shook his head. "No, I have no children." Then his eyes twinkled. "This boy wants tomahawk made so that he could go hunting with brave hunters and kill many buffalo calves."

And it was of vast importance to both the man and the boy, it appeared, that the little tomahawk be made according to the child's own notion of what a tomahawk should be. The handle, like all tomahawk handles, must be of stoutest ash, ending in the usual pipe. But, beneath the pipe, instead of the ordinary hatchet, there was to be a triangle of steel running out to a sharp point.

After a short conference in which the boy, eyes glowing, talked earnestly, A-Leek-Chea-Ahoosh smiled and nodded. He took pencil and paper and drew a design. "Papoose wants it like this," he said.

"But why the sharp point?" Allen inquired.

The Indian chuckled. "So papoose kill many buffalo," he explained.

Then, while the two waited, Allen made the tomahawk. He took great pains with the little toy, using tempered steel for the blade, grinding it to the sharpest of points. A-Leek-Chea-Ahoosh paid for it when it was finished, but Allen received reward of more import to him in the flash of gratitude from two pairs of dark eyes glowing with happiness.

"Bot sots!" the Crow murmured as he placed the tomahawk in the eager hands of his young charge and led him away.

This was at the beginning of the buffalo hunt, in early fall of 1880. Winter set in early that year when, across bleak wind-swept plains no man ventured unless driven by necessity. Once more crowding events drove thought of A-Leek-Chea-Ahoosh from Allen's mind. But an Indian never forgets either an injury or a kindness. One day of late spring the door of the blacksmith shop opened and A-Leek-Chea-Ahoosh walked in, smiling, lead-

ing the same small lad by the hand. Under one
arm the boy was carrying his tomahawk, the handle
adorned with hand-carving and with streamers of
elk hide, fringed and beaded. Under the other arm
was a bulky package. This, with a shy proud smile,
the child offered to Allen. It was a buffalo robe, exquisitely tanned and bleached, made from the hide
of a buffalo calf.

"For our white brother," A-Leek-Chea-Ahoosh
explained. "Papoose kill calf with tomahawk. His
first buffalo. Very proud. Squaw tan it, make it
white, fringe it, for our brother."

After that, for many snows, the young Crow
brave was a frequent visitor at the government
blacksmith shop and he seldom came without some
gift for his friend Allen. Once, Dr. Allen recalls,
it was a purse of elk hide, beautifully beaded, another time a pipe of ash, polished and carved.

And so, slowly, with a trust and a rather pathetic gratitude on the one side and with genuine
admiration on the other, time cemented between
the men a friendship that has endured for fifty
years.

When last they met in the reception room of
Doctor Allen's dental office at Billings, in September of 1931, old Chief Plenty Coups placed a shaking hand on Allen's shoulder and strained his poor
dimmed eyes to see the face of his white brother.
Time has not dealt kindly with this last chief of
the Crows.

"Fifty-four snows ago," he said, in a voice husky and quavering, "we met on the banks of the Little Big Horn. We were boys then, young and strong. After fifty-four snows we are still friends."

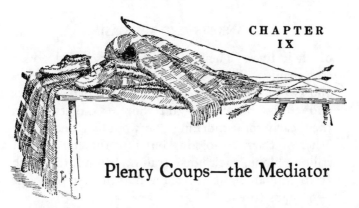

Plenty Coups—the Mediator

WHEN the West was young, Hoskin and Mc-
Girl's trading post, located just below Baker's
Battlefield where the town of Huntley now stands,
was doing a thriving business. It was a horse mar-
ket, a chamber of commerce, a social center, the
Mecca toward which trails of all plainsmen eventually led. Prospectors from the hills came in to toss
down little sacks of gold dust in exchange for bacon
and coffee and flour and sugar so they could go out
into the hills again. Merchants from the East
brought in beads and calico and whiskey. Trappers,
their furs and hides. Indians came with horses to
exchange for other horses and with buffalo and
elk hides to exchange for coffee and calico and beads
and sugar—much sugar.

And the men who trailed in from the lonely
silence of hills and plains to this busy little post
usually lingered there a day or two, stimulated into
an effervescent gayety by the sight of human faces
and the touch of human hands. It meant for them
a brief playtime snatched from out the monotony

of their lives. They exchanged horses and gossip and drinks. They slapped each other's shoulders and swore good-natured oaths. They played poker and threw horseshoes and shot at targets. And then, early some morning you would see one or another of them go jogging out into the eternal vast stillness alone, pack horse trailing behind, to vanish from human sight for three months—six—a year —perhaps forever.

They were making history, those young courageous rugged-faced men disappearing in clouds of alkali dust, though they did not know it then. Among them were such men as Custer and Captain "Yellowstone" Kelly, plainsman and scout, "the little man with the big heart"; and, rarely, such women as Calamity Jane, quick-shooting, harddrinking, warm-hearted.

Doctor Allen recalls one particularly eventful day in the spring of 1879 when the Post was more than usually crowded with palefaces and Indians— Crow Indians—who had brought in a big band of horses for trade or sale, driving them, for the time being, into a corral.

The day began peacefully enough with a feast of barbecued buffalo meat, ending up with buffalo tongues, washed down by much whiskey, of which all partook, both whites and reds. Then, still in genial mood, they played horseshoe, staking blankets and hides on each throw. Later someone set up an empty beer bottle as a target and they gambled

at target-shooting. If a man at sixty yards broke
the bottle he won fifty cents. If he merely chipped
the neck without breaking it he won a dollar. If
he missed entirely he forfeited a dollar.

Many Crow dollars dropped into the pockets of
the whites that day, for the Indian is a notoriously
poor shot with a gun. Bow and arrow in hand he
defies competition, but something about the mech-
anism of a gun seemed always to perplex the red
man. However, this day they took their defeat
with a laugh, for they are true sportsmen; the game
of chance, whether they win or lose, always fas-
cinates them.

Wearying of the beer-bottle game the Crows
announced they had with them one who at long
range could outshoot any man among the palefaces. For the target they chose a certain white
stone on the rimrocks across the Yellowstone five
hundred yards distant.

Tom McGirl called their bet. He said: "I'll bet
a pony we've got a man can beat your Crow."

Promptly an Indian pony and Tom McGirl's
pony were necked and picketed aside.

McGirl turned to Allen. "Here, Doc, you shoot
for me."

Each competitor was to have five shots. The
Crow fired first. His first three shots went close
but a little below the white stone. Like all Indians
he failed to gauge distance accurately. Some
friendly white offered him his whiskey bottle. The

Crow took a long drink, squared himself, aimed carefully, and fired again. His fourth shot went wide the mark, as also his fifth and last. Somewhat discomfited he sought solace in the friendly white man's bottle.

Then Allen leveled his gun and aimed and fired. His first shot and his second and third went wild. The Crows began shouting and slapping one another's backs. They were jubilant.

McGirl's face was flushed. "Say, Doc!" he muttered, anxiously, "what's ailin' you today?"

Allen drew a long breath, pressed his lips tight, and squinted along the barrel of his gun. He understood what the matter was. He had failed to reckon on the exact fall in a five-hundred-yard shot. So he aimed just a little higher this time and fired. The bullet smacked the white stone. He fired again, and again he hit the stone. The Crow pony went to McGirl.

After drinks had been passed around, a Crow who went by the name of "Snow" bet twenty dollars that at twenty yards he could put five shots into a target the size of a half dollar nearer the center than any white man could. Bill Hamilton called his bet. Tom McGirl held stakes. Allen scraped the bark off a pine tree and, with charcoal, marked a black center against the white. The boastful Snow begged for a drink and, having fortified himself for the ordeal, took his rifle, aimed carefully, and fired five shots, two within the black center; three far to one side. Hamilton was not an exceptionally good shot, his fame in the West resting upon his spitting abilities, but this was apparently his lucky day. He leveled his gun and without seeming to aim at all fired five rapid shots, every one of them piercing the black center of the target.

Glumly Snow handed over his twenty dollars. For the Crows, something of the first keen edge of pleasure in gambling was being dulled by their repeated losses. Then, also, the whiskey bottle had been passed around rather too frequently for the good of all concerned. As the day wore on, the Indians were noticed more and more often gathered in groups, muttering among themselves, their small eloquent hands conveying much of their ill-temper in sign talk. Repeated defeats combined with repeated drinks of fire water had aroused the ever slumbering racial antagonism into life.

At an unpropitious moment when overstrained nerves were stretched to the breaking point some bungling fellow came sauntering up from the corral to announce that among the Crow horses down there was one bearing Bill Hamilton's brand. Immediately Bill, with a long string of excited whites and Indians trailing after him, went rushing down to the corral to verify the report. True enough, there was a sorrel bearing the E-Z-Bar brand.

"Say!" Bill yelled, "that there's my horse. Anybody with eyes can see that!"

And he leaped the fence and went over to the horse. But the Indian known as "Snow" was before him. He slung a lariat over the horse's neck and gripped it defiantly. He said he had bought the horse and paid for it. He didn't know a thing about Hamilton's brand, but the horse was his and he refused to give it up. The two men, Bill Hamilton and Snow, stood facing each other, eyes blazing anger. Close to Bill, backing him, were Hi Stewart, Tom McGirl, Liver-eating Johnson and Doc Allen. Aligning themselves with Snow, ready to fight for or with him, were most of the Crow Indians. All the jollity of the day had vanished. Rugged faces were hard, big fists gripped guns and knives. With the suddenness of an electric storm a situation of vast and menacing significance had arisen between whites and reds.

Hi Stewart shouted recklessly, "Take the horse, Bill. It's yours. We'll stand by you."

The Crows said nothing. Their breath was coming in sputtering puffs from between tight-set lips. Their hands felt for the knives at their belts. They were ready to fight to the death for what they deemed their rights.

Allen turned to McGirl. "Say, this is getting serious—" he began, and then paused. "Look! Who's that?"

A man on horseback was coming rapidly toward them from the Post in a cloud of dust. To his unutterable relief Allen recognized his young Crow friend of the plains, A-Leek-Chea-Ahoosh, "the-man-who-makes-many-coups."

Having arrived late at the Post he had just heard of the quarrel between the Crows and the whites. Even before he reached the corral he must have sensed the menace of those two groups of men, the whites on one side, the Crows on the other, with the disputed horse between; he must have caught the defiance in sullen tight-lipped faces, for, as he urged his horse along, he shouted, "Wait!" and held up an arresting hand.

All eyes turned to him. His presence commanded instant attention from both his own people and the whites. In an instant he was off his pony and over the corral fence. Quickly he beckoned for an interpreter and went up to Bill Hamilton.

"You say this is your horse?"

"Yes," said Bill. "It is my horse."

The young Crow turned to Snow. "You say this is your horse?"

"Yes," he muttered, angrily. "I bought it."

A-Leek-Chea-Ahoosh addressed Hamilton. "If this is your horse what proof can you give?"

For answer Hamilton drew a notebook from his pocket and showed his registered brand recorded there. It corresponded to the one on the horse's shoulder.

Then, solemnly, though convinced himself, but so there should remain no doubt in the minds of his people, A-Leek-Chea-Ahoosh drew his knife from his belt and extended it, blade foremost, to Hamilton. "Put your hand on my knife," he directed. "Now, if the horse is yours, if you speak not with crooked tongue, then swear by my knife."

Soberly Hamilton placed his hand on the blade. "I swear," he said, "that the horse is mine."

A-Leek-Chea-Ahoosh nodded. He walked over to the gate and flung it wide. To the Indian, Snow, he said sternly, "Take lariat off white man's horse."

Snow's eyes flashed defiance. Plainly he resented the authority of this man not as large as himself nor as strong, who was not a chief. "I'll not!" he yelled. "The horse is mine. I'll not take the lariat off him."

He was half drunk and fighting mad. He clutched his knife and stood, legs braced, shoulders squared, eyes glittering hate, ready to kill any and every one who should defy him.

Without an instant's hesitation A-Leek-Chea-Ahoosh walked the length of the corral and straight up to Snow, and, while all watched, breathless, the eyes of the two fought a tense, silent battle, fought until Snow's hand dropped listless to his side, and his angry eyes shifted.

Then A-Leek-Chea-Ahoosh jerked the lariat off the horse and tossed it outside the corral. He said to Snow, "Give white man his horse."

With a little gesture of defeat Snow slunk away and Bill Hamilton led his horse out of the corral.

Thus did Plenty Coups in those early days establish his capacity for leadership and his place in the hearts of his white brothers.

Last Great Horse Race
of the Northwest

LIVER-EATING Johnson, Bill Hamilton, Tom
McGirl, and Doc Bill Allen were standing in a
row, boots toed squarely against a straight line
drawn in the dust. On each young weather-beaten
face was the same strained do-or-die expression.

Johnson spit first. His introductory shot hit
the little white stone set up as a target twelve feet
away, but his second merely spattered the dust
near it, while the third went wild. Bill Allen did
no better, and no one was surprised. Neither of
these men claimed to be prize spitters. McGirl
chewed long and vigorously, fixed a determined
eye upon the target, and spit. The first time he
missed by a good six inches. The second shot, however, and also the third, hit the stone.

Two out of three—that was pretty good for
McGirl, but probably not good enough, for Uncle
Bill Hamilton was coming up, and any man competing against Uncle Bill in a spitting contest was
simply handing out donations, bidding "goodbye"

to his dollars before he began. Bill Hamilton was famed as the best spitter in the West.

Bill prepared himself for the ordeal. He jerked up his buckskin pants and pushed his fur cap far back on his shaggy head. He chewed and spit—and hit a cactus four inches from the stone; McGirl gave vent to a guffaw of astonished delight. Hamilton heard that mocking sound and his blood boiled. He took his time, chewed, glared at the little white stone, puckered up his mouth, and tried again. Again he missed and the third time he missed.

Gloomily, in a silence that spoke eloquently of his mortification, he pulled a dollar from his pocket and tossed it to McGirl. The other contestants followed suit.

Allen slapped Hamilton on the back. "What's the matter, old-timer? You don't seem to be up to prime lately."

Bill sighed. Savagely he kicked into the thick alkali dust at his feet. "Naw!" he admitted. "I ain't up to prime. I ain't been up to prime since I lost everything I got to those blasted Crows. Last horse race they took my buffalo hides and my horse and my saddle an' I been walkin' afoot ever since, an' I'm tired, an' I'm broke. That's what's ailin' me."

"Yeah," McGirl admitted, "they know good horse flesh—those blasted Indians. I reckon there ain't nothing traveling on four legs can beat that black of theirs, or Plenty Coups' buckskin."

Just then a man came loitering up to the group. He was a stranger. He said he hailed from Bozeman.

"I overheard what you fellows was saying," he said. "I claim to be the fastest runner in these here parts. I'll bet fifty dollars I can beat any horse living—that buckskin or any other—in a hundred-yard dash, standing start."

Critically they looked him over, a loose-jointed, long-limbed, lanky person, and young, not over twenty-one or two.

"I'll not be betting much money on you, Stranger," Allen remarked, "not against the Crow buckskin, but I'll be hoping you'll win."

"Well," said the stranger, turning away, "any time you say the word I'll be ready. You'll find me up on Sour Dough Creek."

After he strolled away the men discussed the matter. McGirl reasoned that if there wasn't a horse in Montana Territory that could beat Plenty Coups' buckskin how could mere man expect to make a showing. But Allen suggested the man might get a twenty-foot start. "He's got awful long legs," Doc said, "that stranger has." Anyway a race was a race, things had been pretty quiet a long time now, and the restless blood of those Western adventurers thirsted for excitement.

So they spread the news that there was going to be a race, and they sent word to the Crows to bring their buckskin and, on the second day of September almost a half century ago a crowd gathered on the plains along Sour Dough Creek. News traveled with miraculous speed over the vast unpeopled country, and men came pouring in from everywhere. All the men from Hoskins and McGirl's trading post below Baker's Battlefield, men from Mission Creek and Cañon and from Pryor and Big Horn Valley, river men, trappers, scouts, traders, miners and—just adventurers—they all came jogging in to Sour Dough Creek on tired dust-grayed ponies to witness the race between the white man and the famous buckskin horse. And a long procession of Crows came stringing across the prairie, Plenty Coups, a man past thirty then, and behind him many braves on horseback, leading their racing horses.

The very air itself, that balmy fall day out on the prairies of Montana some fifty years ago, was surcharged with a swelling excitement.

The betting, however, proceeded rather listlessly for, while the Crows were eagerly insistent, the whites were cautious. A few ponies were necked along the race track and a few buffalo hides tail-tied, but, for months past the whites had been losing steadily to the Indians and their faith in the long-legged runner from Bozeman was rapidly oozing away.

Across the trail, winding through sagebrush and cactus which tens of thousands of buffalo through countless years had tramped down on their

Crow Belles. Photograph by Goff.

way to water, a rope was stretched. This track, on either side, was bordered thick with excited humans, Indians and whites. The moment came. The lanky stranger pressed against the rope, the dainty buckskin pranced and wheeled and curveted. Then the starter shot his pistol in the air, the rope dropped, and away they went. He was a fast runner, that young man from Bozeman. His thin legs fairly whipped the air, and he began with a few feet advantage. But close at his heels sounded the thud-thud of the horse's hoofs. The man strained every muscle and sinew of his body, his heart pounded stabbingly, his eyes were glued to the goal a short hundred yards distant. The pony crept up and up, ran for a second neck to neck, passed the man in a patter of trim hoofs through the dust, and won the race with an easy two yards to spare.

Naturally the Indians were jubilant. They whooped their joy. Whoever says an Indian never laughs should have seen them that day as they went about, chuckling, collecting their money and necked horses and buffalo hides. The race had made them richer by some eight hundred dollars. They deemed themselves invincible. Nothing, they were convinced, that the palefaces could produce, neither horses nor men, could beat their buckskin or their black. And deep in their hearts they considered the whites fools to keep on trying.

The whites faced their losses with the true

sportsman's good humor. The race had been fair and they had lost—again. That's all there was to it. They all had a barbecue after the race, Crows and whites; they passed the bottle frequently and finished the day spitting at marks, pitching horse-shoes, and shooting at targets.

That day Uncle Bill Hamilton, famous trapper and hunter, famous spitter, recovered his championship title, several dollars, and his self-esteem, for he spit straighter and farther than any other man, Indian or white. Nevertheless, though his pride in his accomplishment had been vindicated, he continued morose.

"How long," he demanded, as he bit off a big chunk of hot savory buffalo meat, "how long is this sort of thing going to go on?"

He, with McGirl and Johnson and Allen, were standing close to the pit where the buffalo had been roasted.

"Are we going to keep right on letting the Crows clean up on us?" he inquired. "I think it's time they was wearing out their moccasins and we was riding our own horseflesh again."

"Well," said McGirl, "if the Crows have got the best horses I don't see's how we can help ourselves."

After that a silence fell upon them. Every one was looking at Bill, for it was apparent by the tense expression of his face that he was mentally debating a weighty question. He sat down cross-legged in the dust and began whittling his finger nails with his hunting knife. He chewed vigorously for a second, and spit, clean and straight and far. Then he spoke.

"Well," he said slowly, "maybe we can't help ourselves, and then again, maybe we can."

"What you got on your mind, Bill?" Liver-eating Johnson inquired.

"Well, I've heard rumors of a horse out in Oregon, name's Snail. Owned by a man named Lankford. I've heard there ain't nothing on four legs can beat it. Maybe Lankford'd come down if we'd make it worth his while."

McGirl was a man of impulse. "I move," he cried, excitedly, "we send someone up there with authority to offer this Lankford five hundred dollars if he'll guarantee to clean up the Crow outfit. It's worth a try."

So, after much heated discussion, while the men sat on the ground eating barbecued buffalo meat, it was decided, and Flappin' Bill was the messenger appointed for the important mission.

"And," Hamilton cautioned, "in the meantime we won't say nothin' to nobody."

Early next morning Flappin' Bill started out. It was a long trip horseback from Bozeman, Montana, out to Oregon. A month might intervene before he could return with Lankford and the wonder horse. During that month the whites were not idle. Having selected the wide stretch of open plain where Columbus, Montana, now stands as the ideal spot for the race, they set to work leveling and packing and widening the old buffalo trail, clearing it of cactus and sagebrush and stones. And while they worked the days lengthened into weeks and one or another was forever pausing to shade his eyes and scan the country to the west for sight of Flappin' Bill.

Now it was four weeks since he started out, now five, and the waiting men were beginning to feel an anxiety they refused to admit. Something, maybe, had happened to Bill. Many things could happen to a lone traveler crossing miles of plains and topping mountains and crossing more plains, riding hour upon hour without sight of human face through a country infested with inimical Sioux and Blackfeet. Maybe he never reached Oregon. Maybe his horse stepped into a prairie dog hole and threw him. There wasn't an hour of any day but someone found an excuse to climb the butte and gaze out toward the western horizon, through air so clear that it carried the vision incredible distances.

The work on the race course was long since finished. It was the beginning of the sixth week and still Flappin' Bill had not returned. Doc Allen took his field glasses and climbed up the butte one fine morning in late October, just, as he casually explained, to see what he might see.

Far to the westward he discerned a speck, dark against the silver-saged plains. The speck moved. It might be grazing buffalo or wild horses. It was advancing steadily. It enlarged. It became men on horses, leading other horses. Allen refocused his glasses. It was Flappin' Bill with a stranger! Then Allen gave one wild whoop and went rolling and sliding down the steep side of the butte and leaped onto his horse and dashed into camp with the news. Flappin' Bill was safe! He was coming home! He had Lankford with him!

At once they hastened to spread the news that a series of horse races would take place on the Yellowstone River about the end of October. And again from hill and river and mountain and plain the whites came straggling in—men—children hungry for thrills. And they brought with them, to bet, everything they owned, all their money, their furs and hides, their horses; for something of the fame of the horse, Snail, had been bruited about among the whites and they stood to win or lose their all on the biggest, most important horse race ever held in the New West.

Over on Pryor Creek the Crow village also was teaming with excitement. Their official crier, wearing his fringed buckskin leggins and red flannel "store" shirt, his black hair in two long thin braids beneath the broad-brimmed hat, had just made the rounds of the tepees and had chanted, solemnly: "The palefaces are going to have a horse race down in the Echeta Casha country. In four sleeps the palefaces will have a race——"

Four sleeps! They must hurry. It would take them all of one sleep to ride down to the white man's valley. What bustle and confusion, what

talk and laughter, what barking of dogs and shouting of children as they prepared for the journey!
At once the women began taking down many of
the tepees and loading them on travois, packing
parfleche boxes with cakes and pemmican and
dried meat and clothing. Into those parfleche
boxes they put all their beautiful trinkets, the
beaded moccasins and belts they had fashioned with
such care during long winter evenings; the polished
and carved bear-tooth necklaces; the festive robes
elaborately adorned with elk teeth; carved tomahawks—all their valued possessions they took along
to bet against the blankets and dollars of the foolish
white men.

Meanwhile the men and the boys rode out onto
the plains and rounded up the horses, some to be
hitched to travois, some to be ridden, some to enter
the races, and many to be necked with the horses of
the palefaces. In those days the Crows were rich
in horses. They caught more than a hundred to
drive down to the race, confident that they would
drive two hundred back home. Had it not been
proved time and again that the whites could not
win?

Finally everything was in readiness for the start.
The last hurried meal had been swallowed, camp
fires tramped out. Young mothers, in their picturesque elk-hide costumes, bright with beads, were
tying babies in softly padded willow-bark cradles.
Older mothers, wearing new calico dresses, were
setting their excited offspring onto ponies. At the

head of the procession, astride horses bedecked with painted feathers, were the solemn chiefs and head-men, patiently waiting. Next came the squaws and children on "squaw" ponies. Then travois for the old ones and other travois with their loads of tepees and provisions. And everywhere, in front and be-hind, and under the feet of the horses, were dogs, sensing a holiday, quite as ecstatic as their masters.

At the very last moment, one of the women screamed, "Wait!" and pointed in dismay to an agitated, forlorn dog, standing at the border of the deserted camp, gazing at them with reproach-ful eyes. The long procession waited.

"She has puppies," the woman cried. "We will be gone many sleeps. We cannot leave her to starve. What can we do?"

No one could think of anything to do. They looked at each other and they looked at the dog, and the dog, wagging a feeble tail, continued to gaze at them imploringly. In her heart a battle evidently waged between maternal duty and in-tense desire.

"Wait!" the woman cried again, this time on a note of triumph. She scrambled off her horse, ran into the tepee and brought out the puppies, four of them. Around each fat little stomach she tied a broad band of soft elk hide. To these bands she fastened thongs and hung them over the back of a pony, so the puppies dangled, two on each side the horse, and thus they rode in comfort all the way, the relieved mother trotting close beside them.

Lankford, with Flappin' Bill, had been at the Post four days now, long enough for his horses to feed and rest.

What a day that was—the day of the race! Winter does not come early to the valley of the Echeta Casha. As far as eye could see the rolling plains were ablaze with the gold of cottonwoods and emerald of pines and crimson of kinnikinnick and silver of sagebrush. The hazy warm air was pungent with the smell of sage and alkali dust and sweaty horseflesh. Everywhere there were dogs and horses and people. White women in crisp calico dresses and sunbonnets, escaping with their husbands from the dreary monotony of life back in the hills, for this rare holiday. Other women, wearing gaudy silk dresses, with painted faces, and without husbands. Trappers and hunters and scouts and traders, tramping about in heavy boots, guns at their belts. Indians. Bucks in moccasins and store pants and bright flannel shirts. Squaws, many young and very pretty, their slender legs and feet trim in beaded moccasins, their gay blankets adding color to the scene.

Hugging the river bank were the Crow tepees. On one side the race track was the white men's corral; on the other, the corral of the Indians.

Immediately the Crows clamored to see the Lankford horses and he led one out, a tall lanky bay. Silently, solemnly, approvingly the Crows looked him over, studied his points, good and bad, drew apart to confer, and then put up their own, a long-legged roan. The two appeared fairly well matched and were put down for a 440-yard run.

And the betting started. Soon big piles of buffalo hides were tailed, and horses—a white man's and an Indian's—were necked. The women, quite as greedy as their bucks, bet their prized jewelry and blankets. Nowhere on earth can there be found a living creature in a higher state of elated bliss than an Indian at a horse race when he is convinced that he is going to win. However, they were not slow in learning that the palefaces, perhaps profiting by previous heavy losses, were a bit cautious in their betting.

Plenty Coups sought his friend Doc Allen. "Bet pony," he offered, "against White Eagle's pony."

"Sure!" Allen agreed, and he necked the loyal, fleet-footed buffalo pony, his comrade in many an adventure over the plains, to Plenty Coups' buckskin. The eyes of the two men met. They smiled their friendship. Plenty Coups stroked the neck of Allen's horse.

"Heap good pony," he said. "Catch plenty buffalo for White Eagle. Now, maybe so, catch plenty buffalo for Indian."

"Maybe so," Allen laughed, "but you fellows can't expect to keep on winning forever."

Chief Iron Bull bet a cherished tomahawk, hand carved and adorned with streamers of beaded elk hide, a thing of beauty, in exchange for a certain buckskin shirt which Hamilton wore on state occasions. It was an elegant garment, that fringed shirt. Long the covetous eye of the Crow chief had been cast upon it. Hamilton called the bet, though with obvious hesitation, and the two articles were cached along with a growing, heterogeneous pile of wagers—garments, moccasins, robes, furs, guns, saddles, and sacks of gold dust— near the track. Thousands of dollars worth of hides and furs were bet by the Crows and called by the whites that November day fifty years ago on the banks of the Yellowstone.

And at last, when the betting began to lag, the two horses, the Lankford bay and the Crow roan, were nosed against the starting rope. They were beautiful animals, both of them. The racing fever was in their blood. They pawed and chafed against the bits, on fire with impatience to be off.

Old Crow, official starter, stood close to the track, waiting for that propitious moment when the two wheeling horses should face toward the goal. Then he pointed his pistol in the air, shouted "Ready!" and fired.

It was a great race. Three-fourths of the way the Lankford horse led, seemingly without effort. Then, surprisingly, almost as though he were being held back, he suddenly lagged behind, straining against the bit, and the Indian roan came in winner by a good ten feet.

The Crows, intoxicated by their victory, and possibly also by the drinks they had been taking from the white man's bottle of fire water whenever it was offered them, yelled themselves hoarse. They

talked fast with tongues, and faster with slim
brown fingers. There were still broad grins on
their faces as they went about collecting their bets.

Plenty Coups led Allen's horse into the corral
with his own. Again he stroked the glossy neck.
"Heap good pony," he gloated. "Maybe so catch
plenty buffalo for Indian."

Glumly Bill Hamilton relinquished his buckskin shirt to Iron Bull. "That's a mighty fine
shirt," he muttered. "It's got long fringe."

Betting on the second race was slower, though
this time it was the Crows who held back. Excited
and jubilant though they were, they had not lost
their natural prudence. The horse Lankford led
out, a proud, spirited creature, all fire and mettle,
they judged to be a faster horse than their own. So,
more times than not, to the whites' insistent challenge, they shook their heads. Having made a
cleaning on the last race, common sense was tem-
pering their gambling frenzy. Although they had
no words for the sportsman's phrase, "the law of
averages," they understood its logic. Sooner or
later they knew that the swing of the pendulum of
chance inevitably carries the victory over to the
other side.

So, having entered their horse, they stood
grouped along the track, watching the race with
the impersonal interest of the born horse-lover.

But, to their unutterable astonishment and dismay, the Lankford horse, for all its speed and
strength, slowed up half way along the track,

dropping back at the finish a neck's length behind the Indian's pony. And again it might have appeared to the discerning eye that he had been held back purposely.

The Crows eyed each other, sadness in their glances. Why had they been afraid to call the white man's bets? Did squaw hearts beat in their breasts? Had it not been proved to them, time after time, that the Great Spirit was with them, His favorite children? Were they not assured that against their strong medicine the palefaces could not win?

Heady all at once with repeated successes, they went swaggering up and down the track, yelling, "Bring on your next horse!"

For this third and final race of the day they of course had reserved their best horse, the famous buckskin, and they reasoned that if the first two could win so easily Buckskin surely had a walk-away. So, "Bring on your next horse!" they kept yelling.

And how they hooted their derision when Lankford did rather shamefacedly lead out the last competitor. It was indeed a sorry creature, dispirited, abject.

"This," Lankford announced, "is my last chance. This is Snail."

Snail was lean and lanky. His coat was shaggy and mud-covered. There were cockleburs in mane and tail. Ambling lazily, he permitted himself to be pulled along, though insisting now and then upon pausing to munch the brown buffalo grass or to cast lethargic glances over the laughing crowd. Perhaps he was wondering why foolish humans spent so much time making loud noises through open mouths when they might be grazing and resting.

If Lankford winked as he introduced Snail to the spectators, the Crows, wrought up to a high tension, gave no heed. They were watching their own sleek buckskin, all decked with vermilion-tinted eagle feathers, as he danced out onto the track. He pawed the dust daintily and snorted scorn at the listless meek-eyed Snail.

And now it required no urging to persuade the Indians to bet. They had learned their lesson. Their eyes glittered, their hands shook as they staked all their worldly goods upon this third race. Every horse in the corral, valuable furs and hides, knives, moccasins, they pressed upon the whites, clamorously. And the whites called their bets.

Lined up with their bucks, the squaws laughed until the tears rolled down their faces at the absurd Snail, dirty, drooping, stolidly munching grass. "Snail!" The name was a joke and the horse was a joke, and the race, in their minds, was already won.

"Squaw pony!" they jeered. "Squaw pony!" And the hot gambling delirium gripped them. Frantic with anticipatory joy they jerked off blankets and bet them, and their copper jewelry and bear-tooth necklaces and beaded moccasins and fringed leggins. Bet with the white men, blankets against sacks of sugar, pony against pony, trinkets

against paleface flour. And the palefaces grinned
and called their bets.

However, beneath the badinage, the good-
natured oaths and laughter, the free exchange of
drinks, ran an undercurrent of strong deep emotion. Everyone sensed that this was to be more
than an ordinary horse race, the best horse to win.
A faint pulse of animosity was throbbing between
the red men and the white.

McGirl pulled Allen aside. He was breathing
hard. "What—" he inquired, huskily, "just what
do you really think of Snail, Bill?"

"Bet all you've got," Allen replied, tersely.

"Maybe—maybe we'll be caught holding the
sack, Bill. Snail looks like a mighty fast horse, still
we don't know——"

"We don't *know* the sun'll shine tomorrow
morning. There might be an eclipse or something."

"I lost my buckskin shirt to Iron Bull," Hamilton muttered. " 'Spose I can win it back?"

"Take a chance," Allen advised.

He elbowed his way through the crowd, searching for Plenty Coups, and found the young subchief on the race track.

"White Eagle wants his horse back," he told
Plenty Coups. "White Eagle bets his big white bear
skin against Billy."

Soberly Plenty Coups shook his head. "Snail no
good," he warned his friend, generously. "Snail
squaw pony. Buckskin bot sots. White Eagle lose."

But Allen pressed upon the Crow the skin of

the grizzly which, when he had shot it, won for him the name "White Eagle." "I'm betting this," he insisted, "against my horse."

Other far more important bets were made. A man from the Big Hole country staked a string of twenty horses against an equal number of the Crows' and his bet was called. A prospector from the hills pulled a little elk-hide sack from his pocket. "This is filled with gold nuggets," he yelled, waving the sack wildly in the air. "I'm betting it on Snail."

Promptly Bell Rock held up ten fingers and pointed to the corral. "Naw!" scoffed the stranger. The Indian indicated fifteen horses. He was eager, confident. And still the stranger shook his head. Twenty! The young Crow desired very much to possess some of the white man's gold.

"Called!" said the prospector. "Here you, Liver-eating Johnson! Hold stakes!" And he tossed the little sack into Johnson's hands.

When the brisk betting had dawdled down, after everything from horses to moccasins had been wagered on the final race, then Lankford, brush and flannel rag in hand, sauntered over to Snail and began grooming him. Instantaneously, before the astonished eyes of the Indians, a metamorphosis no less than miraculous occurred. With burs removed from mane and tail and with his coat shining like burnished copper, Snail, the phlegmatic, became Snail, the mettled aristocrat, a formidable rival even for the Crows' prized buckskin.

Snail's very manner changed. Presumably humiliated by his slovenly appearance, drooping under the derisive hoots of the humans, he had been suffering an equine inferiority complex. Now, cockleburs and mud removed, all his self-abasement vanished. He tossed his head, flaunted his shining beauty, and whinnied a ringing challenge: "Let's get going! What we waiting for?"

He resented the indignity of being bridled, and cavorted his displeasure. He was also displeased when he felt the little jockey on his back. But, quickly, before he could rear, a surcingle was thrown over horse and rider, and drawn tight, binding them together. Whatever the fate of the one it was to be shared by the other. And then Snail did rear and snort and plunge. He pawed the air with protesting front hoofs. He meditated falling over backwards, but, at the crucial moment, when the rider was hovering between life and death, decided against it.

The white men, lined up on one side of the track, were grinning delightedly, but the Crows, opposite, only looked at each other dumbly. On their faces was an expression of amazement and incredulity and smoldering anger. Up and down the line they were grunting, "Pony bot sots!"

Though they still retained faith in the speed of their own buckskin they resented the silly trick that had been played on them. The friendly rivalry of early afternoon vanished completely. More than ever this was to be a tribal race—another unfair conflict between whites and reds.

The two horses were being held, snorting, against the starting rope. The Indian jockey leaped onto his pony and clung there, fumbling prayerfully at the little rawhide sack tied round his neck. In that sack were his beaver foot and bit of otter skin and sparrow-hawk wing, all his strong medicine and all the strong medicine of his tribe, enough, surely, to give him the victory.

The dancing horses faced the goal, the men at their heads leaped back, Old Crow fired his pistol, the rope was dropped and they were off! What a race! The Indian horse started out with a nose-lead advantage. For a second—a second and a half—he kept that lead. The Crows let out one wild whoop of joy, a yell that died strangling in their throats. Snail was creeping up and up, an inch, another, and another. Now, the two were running neck and neck and their nostrils quivered and their eyes were red and their hoofs were sending up sprays of alkali dust.

Again and again the Indian jockey quirted his pony. He managed to squeeze out of the panting little creature another and last burst of speed. Buckskin gained an inch and lost it.

Snail needed no urging. He wasn't running. He was flying through the air in long leaps that sent him ahead twenty-six feet at a bound.

A prolonged moment's torturing anxiety, a moment's strained waiting and watching, and then, in another second it was all over. Snail crossed the line a good ten feet ahead of the laboring little buckskin. The palefaces had won the race!

Gleefully the whites went collecting their spoils. You saw them everywhere, broad grins on their faces, arms full of blankets and knives and moccasins and guns and saddles, bear-tooth necklaces around their necks.

One hundred and sixty horses changed hands that day, some two thousand dollars, and more than two hundred buffalo hides.

Gravely Plenty Coups relinquished to his friend Allen the bear skin and the buffalo pony, Billy. The Indian's eyes were perplexed, troubled.

"White Eagle," he said, "Crow friend. But Snail no squaw pony. Snail thunder horse."

If Plenty Coups resented what savored to his simple mind of treachery, if he felt his friendship betrayed, he made no other intimation, nor did he ever again refer to the matter.

But one little woman in the bright calico dress she had made for the occasion tugged persistently at her man's arm. Her tanned face within the slatted sunbonnet was soft with pity.

"The squaws are crying, Jake," she whispered. "I seen them over in their tepees crying because they've got to walk all the way home and carry their babies."

She said the same thing to McGirl and Hamilton and Johnson and Allen. She talked until she made the jubilant thoughtless man-children see things her way. And then she led them across the plains to the banks of the Yellowstone where the weeping squaws had sought refuge in their tepees. She saw to it that all the trinkets and blankets were returned to the Crow women.

And still she eyed the men sternly. "They'll have to walk home. What you going to do about that?"

For answer the men went to the corral and led out fifteen ponies and gave them to the squaws.

The Crows smiled once more. Something of the bitter tang was washed from their resentful hearts. Perhaps, after all, the palefaces talked once, and were brothers, and meant not to play unfair.

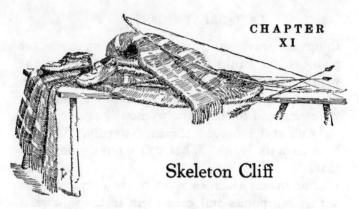

Skeleton Cliff

ABOVE the town of Billings, Montana, and overlooking all the beautiful valley of the Yellowstone with its houses clustered thick, its winding river, its wheat and bean and beet fields, towers a butte known as "Skeleton Cliff."

That shale-ribbed butte, tipped by its groves of pine trees, is a tome, each tree and rock a page upon which have been recorded the tragedies of a vanished race of Indian braves and the adventures of frontiersmen, many of whom followed the buffalo trail to their undoing.

On or near the butte, for the past two hundred years, have occurred repeatedly the momentous events that have made Montana history. Above it looms "Kelly Mountain," on whose topmost peak is the grave of Captain Kelly, "The Little Man With The Big Heart," who spent the daring young years of his life making of the valley a safe abode for coming generations. He knew this country when it was hideous with the war cry of Indians, and when its breast was dyed red by the blood of

the hunted buffalo and by the blood of the whites
and the reds who battled for supremacy over the
contested land.

Farmers have supplanted hunters and warriors.
Wheat fields cover the buffalo trail that Kelly followed so often on his jogging Indian pony. Auto-
mobile highways circle hills that but half a century ago served as ambush for lurking Blackfeet
and Sioux, ready with bow and arrow. And Kelly
sleeps his last sleep above that valley where, so he
tells us, he spent the happiest years of his life as
plainsman and scout, the valley he helped prepare
for civilization.

On another butte above Skeleton Cliff, to the
right of Kelly Mountain, stands the monument of
another plainsman, still living, Bill Hart. Immor-
talized in bronze, he leans against his horse, Paint,
and rolls a cigarette as he gazes out across the valley
where his adventurous youth was spent.

Below Skeleton Cliff, just across the winding
road that was once a buffalo trail leading from
the plains over rimrocks and through Alkali Pass
to the Yellowstone River, is "Boothill" Cemetery.
The low hill is dotted with the graves of Dan Lahey,
Bill Preston, Muggins Taylor, Dave Courier—all
those hot-headed, quick-shooting, dare-devil man-
children who challenged death with every breath
they drew and loved the tonic sense of danger.

When Doctor Allen—young Doc Allen then—
first came to the Yellowstone Valley and set up a

dental-barber-blacksmith shop, Kelly was dashing gayly over the plains from Yellowstone River to Cañon Creek, hunting, scouting, and incidentally putting the fear of the law into the hearts of wild red men. There was no Billings. The town of Coulson on the south bank of the Yellowstone was in its infancy and its enterprising citizens were bemoaning the deplorable fact that their town could not boast a cemetery because, as yet, no one had died.

"And," they argued, sadly, "a town ain't a real town without a cemetery."

Their discontent, however, soon ceased to find cause upon which to thrive, for, in the midst of their grumbling, John Alderson killed Dave Courier in a quarrel concerning squatter rights. And those same men who had bemoaned the lack of a graveyard bore Dave very tenderly up to the low hill just below Skeleton Cliff and buried him there, with his boots on. A long line of mourners, roughly clad, heavily booted, stood with heads bared reverently, an expression of solemnity on their weather-beaten faces, while clods of dirt fell upon what had once been "Dave." Bill Hamilton was there and Ed and Charlie Newman, Muggins Taylor, Skookum Jo, Sam Alexander, and Bud McAdow, their boisterous high spirits hushed by this first visit of Death.

The town of Coulson had its graveyard, and the famous "Boothill" cemetery its first victim.

At that time, just above the hill with its one lonely grave, was a clump of pine trees clinging to the shale ribs of Skeleton Cliff. Often, from the door of his shop in Coulson, Doc Allen had noticed hawks and crows hovering thick above that spot. And when there was a breeze, he saw long streamers of gaudy hue floating out from the pines. Finally, his curiosity sufficiently aroused, Allen crossed the river in his boat and climbed the rimrock to that particular clump of pine trees on Skeleton Cliff which held such attraction for the birds.

He peered up into the branches, to shrink back from the sight confronting him. It was a ghastly joke that while the town of Coulson had been lamenting its dearth of dead men these trees were drooping under the weight of their dead.

For each tree there was one skeleton or more, perhaps a hundred all told, seeming to grin with ghoulish mirth as they dipped and swayed and rattled their bones, dangling from branches in the breeze. Bright blankets had apparently been used as shrouds, swathing the bodies, and these blankets, rotted and torn to shreds by time and weather, floated like gay banners through the air.

The bodies, Allen perceived, had been bound to the trees with tough rawhide thongs, but the thongs too were beginning to rot, sometimes releasing a bleached skeleton so that it dangled from the branches as though it were dancing to the tune of the wind.

Scattered on the ground beneath the pines were brass and copper rings, polished elk-tooth necklaces, feathered head-pieces, beaded moccasins and belts, tomahawks—all the cherished trinkets of a people that had been childishly vain, royally proud, vitally alive.

Allen's interest was aroused. Often he had seen the bodies of Indians laid to rest in trees or on scaffolds or in crevices in rocks, but only one or two in a place. For so many in this spot he could not account. He was convinced that back of the mystery there must be a story. Persistently, after that, he plied everyone he met, both whites and reds, with questions. Though many palefaces had seen the skeletons in their aerial sepulcher none could explain their presence there. If the Indians knew they refused to tell.

It was not till some two years after his discovery that Allen's curiosity was satisfied. Then, one night as he and Plenty Coups lay stretched by a camp fire on the plains after a hard day's elk hunt, the young Indian told a tale of his people. In that tale or legend may lie the solution to the mystery that has made of Skeleton Cliff a point of historic interest.

"I tell White Eagle a story as my uncle told it to me," he said. "Many snows ago there was a branch of River Crows who were big men, heap tall, heap strong. It is said of them that they were all over six feet tall and that they had hair reaching the ground. They were very proud of their long hair. In battle or on the hunt they wore it braided and wrapped round their heads, but when idling about camp they let it hang loose. They were brave warriors. They were to our people what Custer's men were to the whites, always guarding us from enemies. They had no squaws. Their tepees were set at the foot of the cliff now known as Skeleton or Sacrifice Cliff. From there they could see all the wide plain below, could see enemies from far off. These Crow braves had six-foot bows made of mountain ash with tough sinews glued along the back to strengthen them. And their arrows were long and flint-pointed and very sharp.

"For many snows those big warriors lived their lives upon the peak close to the Blue and guarded the Crow villages down in the valley. They were young and strong and knew no fear, and their hearts sang all day long. At night their camp fires could be seen leaping up into the trees and their songs could be heard all over the valley. In their camps, and in the camps of all their people, were always many buffalo tongues and much dried elk meat and buffalo meat. Over their heads the pines sang to them. At their feet ran the waters of the Echeta Casha. And the stream of life flowed swift and warm in their veins.

"Though they had heard of a strange sickness that was taking Sioux and Blackfeet tribes as far down as the Missouri, yet they felt no fear, for the Great Spirit had been very kind to His Crow children. He would let no harm come to them. They were strong with the strength of youth; they were strong like the sapling that bends but does not break; they were strong like the bow that is stretched only to spring back into place.

"Then, after one sleep, so my uncle told me, there was a warrior who could not rise from his bed of buffalo hides. His limbs were heavy and tired and, when he tried to stand, were weak like the limbs of a sick squaw, so that he sank down again. His eyes were dimmed, his body ached, and his throat burned for water. When he called for water, and others hearing him went into his tepee, they saw that upon his face and his body were red spots. Those spots stung like the sting of a bee. In his heart and in the hearts of all who saw him was fear.

"Quickly they built a sweat lodge, and, heating stones to a white heat, poured water over them until the lodge was filled with steam. Then they carried the sick warrior into the lodge so that the evil spirits should all be sweated away. When he was wet with sweat they carried him down to the Echeta Casha and bathed him in the cold water. But nothing they did was good. Though they called loudly upon the Great Spirit He did not seem to hear them. For many sleeps the medicine men gathered in the tepee of the sick man and danced and sang and beat their tom-toms close to him, but even they could not drive out the evil spirits. In spite of all that was done for him the young brave left his earthly home and was taken across the Slippery Log to the Happy Hunting

Ground. Then they wrapped him in a blanket and bound him to a tree on the side of the cliff. Near him they tied all the things he loved best, his war bonnet and tomahawk and war club. Beside him they also placed dried meat. And they killed his horse and left it on the ground below him, for he would need all those things on his journey.

"Soon another warrior was stricken, and another, and still another, until over the entire hunting village hung a great fear of the evil spirit that was painting the faces of the warriors with ugly red marks, as though they were preparing for battle, and was making them weak, with feet that stumbled, like one who had drunk of the white man's fire water. It seemed that neither their strong medicine nor the wise medicine men with their dances and yells and bag of charms, nor even the Great Spirit could help them. The sick warriors crept into the sweat lodges and took sweat baths, and then, while their blood flowed like streams of fire through their bodies, bathed in the icy waters of the river. To many of them came terrible visions, so that they talked strange talk. Many of them, unable longer to endure the suffering, plunged knives into their hearts. And with every sleep another brave died, and another.

"The sick ones begged the strong ones to leave before they also were stricken down. But Crows do not desert their sick brothers. And when the sick ones died the strong ones carried them out of their tepees, wrapped them in blankets, and bound them to trees, there to sleep their last sleep. Very soon, on the bodies of the strong would come those strange red marks, and the fire in the veins, and the aching head and burning thirst. Then they too took sweat baths and plunged into the cold river and staggered back to their beds in their tepees, never to rise again.

"We know now that they did the wrong thing, but they did not know then and there was no one to tell them. We know now that the palefaces call that strange sickness 'smallpox.' We have been told that many snows ago a paleface miner was drifting down the Echeta Casha where it enters into the Missouri at the Fort called 'Union.' Suddenly this strange sickness came upon him, out there alone. He paddled to shore and took off his clothes, for his body burned, and he longed for the touch of cold water. He bathed in the river and then he lay down under the trees. An Indian of the Blackfeet tribe found him there dead and took his clothes and put them on and rode into his village. Soon most of the Blackfeet were sick and many of them died, and then the Sioux, and finally the great Crow warriors.

"My uncle told me," Plenty Coups went on, "that while a few of the Crow braves were yet strong they erected a big mound of stones, four feet wide and sixteen long, so that as long as a stone should rest upon a stone, people of snows not yet fallen might see and know of the evil that had come into the camp of our people.

"And then," Plenty Coups said, "as to what follows, some tell one story and some another. It has been said that when there were only sixteen warriors left of the many, then, because they knew that in their veins ran the evil which had destroyed their brothers, and because they feared the evil spirit might soon destroy all the Crow tribe, they gathered around the camp fire one night in council. Their hearts were heavy. They smoked the medicine pipe and the wise ones spoke.

" 'We can never return to our people,' one of them said. 'The sickness which took our brothers is also in us. It is better that sixteen braves die than that the great nation of Crows be destroyed. I have spoken.'

" 'Our brother speaks well,' another said. 'His tongue is not crooked. We are weary. Our hearts have ceased to sing. Never again shall we find joy in the hunt nor in war dances nor in feast days. We are like old, old men. Let us seek peace in the Happy Hunting Ground.'

"And, so it is said, those sixteen braves rode their horses up onto the top of that butte which is highest in all the valley and drove them over and down onto the sharp rocks below. And there they died together, the young braves and their horses.

"But the story as my uncle told it is like this: When the great band of warriors had been taken until only sixteen were left, then all the happiness went out of their hearts. It seemed to them very still in the big camp where all had been laughter and shouts and dancing and songs. No longer did they feel joy in hunting the buffalo, for few were left to eat even the buffalo tongues, yellow with fat. When they walked, they walked like old, old men, nor were their feet light in the tribal dances. When they spoke to the Great Spirit their words did not reach up into the Blue. The song of the wind in the pine trees was a sad song now, sounding to them like the voices of their comrades who had been called away across the Log. And when the sun fell down behind the rimrocks it left a heavy, thick darkness that seemed filled with evil spirits, and they were afraid, so few in all the black, silent loneliness. Nothing could ever again be as it had been.

"One night as they sat around their camp fire, while the darkness, peopled with evil ones crept closer and closer to them, the headman spoke: 'For some cause which we do not understand,' he said, 'the Great Spirit is angry with His children the Crows. When we pray to Him, He does not hear. Though we have danced and chanted our medicine songs and beat the tom-toms, yet we have not done enough. Something more is wanted of us by the Great Spirit. He demands a sacrifice, the greatest in our power to give. Let us say to Him that we will give our lives if He will grant once more to our people health and strength and happiness. But let us ask for a sign so that we may know our words have been heard. We will prepare for death. We will chant our death songs. Then, if our sacrifice seems good to the Great Spirit He will make the fire leap higher than the tallest tree. If not, then the fire shall die down. I have spoken.'

"So they gathered pine branches and built a great fire. Then they dressed in their war costumes and painted their faces and danced round the fire, singing their songs and watching the flames. The fire burned brighter and leaped higher until it reached far above the tallest tree.

"The headman pointed to the flames. 'The Great Spirit has heard our words,' he said. 'That is His promise that He will smile again upon our people.'

"Then the sixteen young warriors blindfolded their horses and mounted them and drove them along the buffalo trail until they came to a high point overlooking the river. The headman gave the sign. Together they struck their horses with quirts so that the animals went plunging and screaming over the edge and their hoofs clung to the stones and the soft shale gave way and they and their riders went down, many hundreds of feet, into the Echeta Casha.

"The braves had made their last journey along the dark trail. They had given their lives so that the Great Spirit should once more be kind to His children the Crows. And," Plenty Coups added, gravely, "White Eagle knows that He has been kind."

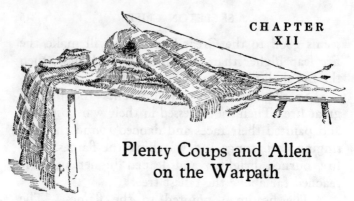

Plenty Coups and Allen
on the Warpath

(Excerpt from Dr. Allen's Journal. Sept. 19, 1880.)

EARLY yesterday morning I went to the corral
to turn my team of oxen and my saddle horse,
Prince, out to graze. I've been shutting them up
nights, with Nero on guard, ever since the Blackfeet got away with my six horses.

Morning is the best time of the day. It seems
good then just to be alive and young, and I guess
Prince thought so too. He managed to look foolish,
kicking up his heels and acting like a frisky colt
around the corral. Then he came crowding
against me, head hanging over the gate, gazing
sort of wistful across the range. I didn't blame
him. I understood that longing in his eyes. I
ached to be out there too, cantering miles and
miles across the open. I guess it's in the blood of all
Westerners, both horses and men, to fret against
being penned up.

In the fall I believe our Yellowstone Valley is
about the prettiest sight in the world. There'd been
a heavy frost the night before and hills and rim-

rocks were a glossy brown, coated with silver. Wild rose bushes and kinnikinnick looked like splashes of fire, and down in the coulees cottonwood trees were gold.

As I was standing there at the corral gate, just looking, with Prince nosing my shoulder, I heard a great hullabaloo up at the house, clatter of horses' hoofs and men's voices—Indians I knew them to be at once. So I hurried around to the front of the cabin without turning Prince loose, which was lucky for me.

I could tell by the heaving sides of the horses that the Indians had been riding hard. They were all excited. One of them rushed up to me.

"Are you Sioux?" I asked.

He shook his head and, pulling off his hat, pointed to his hair. It was roached, so I knew he was a Crow.

Then the man in the lead stood up in his stirrups and I recognized my old friend Plenty Coups. I shook hands with him and invited him into the house but he shook his head. He explained to me quickly in sign language: "Blackfeet stole twenty Crow horses last night and crossed Yellowstone."

"In which direction did they head?" I asked.

He turned and looked north and pointed to Lake Basin. Although Plenty Coups doesn't speak English and I don't know much about Crow yet he and I have good times together and understand each other. I manage the sign language as well as most Indians.

He told me the horses had been stolen from the Crow camp the night before and he was going after them and wanted me to go along. Time was when he wouldn't have asked help of any one, but since the white man has begun to rule the plains, making horse-thieving a criminal offense, Plenty Coups guards against misunderstandings, often by inviting some of his white brothers to accompany him on raids such as this. The man doesn't know the meaning of the word "fear," but he's a shrewd diplomat.

There was nothing I wanted more than to catch that bunch of thieving Blackfeet. It wasn't more than a month ago that one of them had stolen my six horses, including the pony Pretty Eagle had given my son Willie. Of course Plenty Coups brought the pony back to us, and a few days later the body of the Blackfeet was found across the Yellowstone close to William Roger's cabin with three bullet holes through his body. But that hadn't stopped the thieves. Every day some settler reported horses or cows missing. One night Brockway woke up with a glare of light in his window. He looked out and there was the big stack of wild hay he'd put up for the winter all ablaze. And Irwin had four piles of buffalo boss ribs and a sack of flour taken from his lean-to. Everybody laid it all to a thieving gang of Blackfeet.

So I said, "You bet I'll go. I'll get a bunch together and we'll take the trail up over the Hogback
and cut due north until we cross your trail or meet
the Blackfeet. You fellows go round by Alkali Flat
and head for Hailstone Basin."

The Crows wheeled their horses and galloped
away. I saddled Prince and went around getting
together a few of the boys. I routed out Bill Brockway, Gene Irwin, and Charley Demaris and we
rode up over the Hogback into Lake Basin. I
thought maybe as soon as we got up on the flats we
would see the Crows coming from Alkali.

You get a clean view up in Lake Basin country
—miles and miles without tree or bush, stretching
on to rimrocks that edge the horizon. Yesterday
morning it was cold and tingly. The air up there
was sort of spicy with frosted sagebrush and greasewood. You can't get enough of it; you gulp it in
and it goes racing through your veins, making you
feel like a ten-year-old. A flock of wild geese flew
over our heads, going south. Demaris sighted into
the bunch, but the rest of us knocked his gun
down. We asked him if he wanted to advertise our
trip to the Blackfeet. Up on Antelope Point we
saw some antelope. The pretty little fellows peeked
down at us sort of curious, ready to run at the first
hint of danger. By that time it was near noon.

Demaris smacked his lips. "Um, boys! Antelope
steak sizzling over a fire!"

"Yes!" Brockway said, "and tonight our scalps hanging on Blackfeet scalp poles!"

So we just rode along, chewing dried elk meat. For a long time we didn't see a sign of the enemy, no signs of life at all except meadow larks and prairie dogs and rabbits. Then Brockway exclaimed, "What's that?" and pointed in the direction of Rattlesnake Butte.

Something over there was stirring up great clouds of dust. We thought maybe it was Blackfeet with the band of stolen horses. Our hands went to our guns, but pretty soon a big bunch of buffalo came thundering past us and they weren't heading for Alkali Pass that opens up the way to the Yellowstone, for water. They acted excited, as though something had frightened them.

"I bet where they started from is where the Blackfeet are now," I said.

So I got out my field glasses and climbed Antelope Point. From there I could see every foot of the Lake Basin plains and soon I spied a camping outfit at the base of Rattlesnake Butte, close to Big Lake. They had a lot of horses and I felt pretty sure they were the Blackfeet we were after. In a little while along came Plenty Coups and his four men from Alkali. I told him what I'd seen.

He smiled and nodded. "Heap good!" he said. "White Eagle talk with straight tongue. White Eagle Crow friend. Our horses tired. Blackfeet horses tired, maybe so. We rest now and tonight we fight our enemy and get our horses."

We sure were tired. It was now late afternoon.
We'd been riding since early morning; it was a stiff
climb up over the Hogback and Rattlesnake Butte
was still a good ten miles away. I told them I knew
where there was water and so we circled Antelope
Point and came to a deep coulee cutting into the
butte where there was a spring and plenty of grass
and where, most important of all, the smoke from
our camp fire couldn't be seen by the Blackfeet.

Gene Irwin had been leading a pack horse all
the way and the rest of us had been poking fun at
him. But now, while some unsaddled the horses and
some gathered buffalo chips for our fire, Gene began unpacking. He had bread and chocolate cake
—mashed a bit and crumbly but looking mighty
good to us—and a pot to boil coffee and a great big
chunk of fresh buffalo meat.

Demaris got excited right away. He was all for
digging a pit and lining it with red-hot stones and
roasting the meat. Nothing in all the world tastes
better than tender buffalo meat edged round with
fat, barbecued in a pit. But it's a slow process and
we were all too hungry to wait. So Demaris, as
usual, was voted down. Instead, we cut branches
from sagebrush and fastened chunks of meat on
them and broiled them over the fire. My, it tasted
good, along with bread and hot coffee! And that
cake! Right away we voted Irwin's wife the best
cook in Yellowstone Valley.

After our feed most of us stretched round the

fire, smoking—not talking, not thinking much—
just feeling. The sun slipped behind Battle Butte.
It got cooler so that the warmth of the fire felt
good to us, but, down in the coulee, the wind didn't
hit us. How quiet it was. No sound but the horses
cropping grass and now and then a sleepy meadow
lark, and maybe a prairie dog chattering. While
over our heads, up on the plains, the wind came
creeping, creeping, through the prairie grass, with
a soft, steady, swishing sound.

I glanced at Plenty Coups and his eyes met mine
and he smiled. I wished I could read his thoughts.
He has the soul of a poet. I knew he was feeling
the beauty same as I was.

We were going into battle. We were about to
fight a bunch of lawless, desperate Blackfeet.
Maybe all of us wouldn't live to get back down
into the valley. But I'm safe in saying not one of
us gave a thought to danger. We were just living
the hour we were sure of.

Plenty Coups had sent a couple of wolves up
onto the Point to scout around. We'd forgotten
about them until we heard the chink of stones
slipping down the butte. Then we all leaped to
our feet in a jiffy, wide awake, hands to our guns.
But it was the two Crow scouts. They reported
that the Blackfeet hadn't moved from their camp
on Big Lake. They had the horses bunched below
Rattlesnake Butte with just one man guarding
them.

Plenty Coups was excited. "Come!" he said, and in a second he had caught his horse and was mounted, ready to start. The rest of us weren't long behind. Part of the way we could circle buttes or ride along the bottom of coulees, out of sight, but the last five miles we had to travel pretty much in the open. If the Blackfeet felt any suspicion they were being followed or if they had wolves posted on buttes—well, next morning there'd be another grave or so in Boothill cemetery.

At first the moon shone full and bright, making the whole Lake Basin flat light as day, but after a bit it slid under a cloud, for which kindness we were duly grateful.

We rode single file, Plenty Coups taking the lead, and we never spoke a word, and you couldn't hear a sound except the creak of saddles and the muffled clump of horses' feet through thick grass and our own quick breathing. All the time we rode with one hand on the reins and the other on our guns, ready to fire or to wheel and run, whichever seemed the most sensible thing to do.

Riding so quiet and slow—it took us about an hour to make the last five miles—we came to within a hundred yards of the Blackfeet camp. We could see the dark blur of it against the silver-frosted plains. We could see the big bunch of horses and the one man keeping them together, riding round and round, a ghostly figure in the dim light.

Plenty Coups motioned for us to stop. He got down off his horse without making a sound and went slithering through the grass on hands and knees, inching his way along slowly toward the lonely rider. In another second he would have reached him and could have struck him with his war club, but just then some one in our line—I'm sure it was Demaris, although he's denied it—let out a sneeze. In all my life I've never heard anything so loud as that sneeze exploding through the hushed, waiting, dark silence.

Immediately things began to happen. We saw the surprised Blackfeet wheel his horse and aim his gun straight down at the crouching Plenty Coups, but before we could go to his aid the whole camp was awake and rushing us. The night stillness of the plain was broken by trampling horses and shouts and shots and moans.

We were about equally divided, eight Blackfeet to eight whites and Crows. I can't describe the battle in detail, although, as long as I live, I'll hear the whistling of men breathing through their clenched teeth, and see white desperate faces. It was a man-to-man fight, each for himself. I was too busy to know how the others were faring. A big Blackfeet came leaping towards me, getting bigger every second. In the dim light he looked to be about fifteen feet tall. I aimed at him and fired and missed. He fired at me and missed. The next second he had dragged me off my horse and we were rolling on the ground, locked tight in each other's arms, he trying to hit me with his war club, I trying to get at his throat.

I'm a big man myself, and considered pretty strong, but that Blackfeet had me beat. The fight seemed to go on and on into the centuries. I could feel my strength oozing away. It seemed that every sinew in my body was being torn out. My breath was getting short. I knew I couldn't hold out much longer. I fought on, thinking, though, it wouldn't be such a bad thing to die, so's I could rest awhile. I felt a dull thud from a war club on my head, not very hard at such close quarters, just enough to make me feel woozy and relax my hold. I saw stars; I was expecting another finishing blow, when all of a sudden the Blackfeet giant crumpled down beside me and lay still. I glanced up. There was Plenty Coups, war club in hand, smiling his calm smile. He had saved my life.

By the time I got to my feet and looked around, still dazed by the blow on my head, the fight was about over. Things began to clear for me. I saw dead bodies—horses and men—scattered about. I saw Brockway crouching back of his fallen horse, aiming at a shadow running back of the butte. I aimed and fired and the shadow threw up its hands and fell face forward. That was the last of the Blackfeet horse thieves.

Not one of our party was seriously wounded. One of the Crows was shot in the hand; Irwin's left arm dangled loose; Brockway had his horse shot from under him, and my head ached and felt as big as a barrel, but that was all. We considered ourselves pretty lucky. And were the Crows happy!

In a short time we had rounded up the twenty-five stolen horses—some of them had stampeded miles across the plains—and then we all started back past Antelope Point and down the Hogback to the valley, driving the riderless horses ahead of us. The Crows had Blackfeet scalps dangling at saddle horns. Some of them had made coup. They began to sing one of their wild war songs. It sounded uncanny way out there on the night-shrouded plains and made chills go up and down my spine, but somehow it sounded beautiful too.

I didn't know the Crow words but I joined in: "Hey-ya! Hey-ya! Hey-i-a-a-a!"

So did Brockway and Irwin and Demaris, until the voices of all of us—Crows and whites—rang through the darkness and echoed and re-echoed against all the buttes. It was as though our voices had been balls and the buttes giants, tossing them back and forth.

It was morning when we got back into Yellowstone Valley. The Crows made camp on the banks of the river and set up a scalp pole and they and all their people had a scalp dance and a feast that lasted all that day and all the next night.

We palefaces didn't put on any celebration after our victory but we are glad just the same, for we've taught the Blackfeet horse thieves a lesson they're not likely to forget in a hurry. Maybe, now, our horses and cattle will be safe out on the range.

I went to bed, for my head was buzzing and throbbing. As I drifted off to sleep I could see a confused mass of shadowy figures milling about, leaping, struggling, running, and in the blurred picture the face of Plenty Coups with that quiet shining smile. What a friend an Indian is to a man when he is a friend!

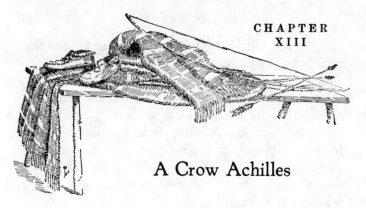

A Crow Achilles

TROUBLE ON CROW RESERVATION!

AGENT H. E. WILLIAMSON THREATENED WITH DEATH! TROOPS CALLED OUT FOR PROTECTION!

THESE startling headlines appeared in the Billings *Gazette,* under date of October 2, 1887. And that date marks the beginning of a month of turmoil in Montana Territory, a month darkened by fear and hatred and tragedy.

The trouble, set in motion by so trifling an incident as the looting of horses by young Crow braves from their enemy the Blackfeet, hinged upon the varying interpretations of their imprudent act. The whites said the horses were stolen, and horse thieves, in the early days of the lawless West, were shown little mercy. The Crows maintained that the horses were lawful plunder taken from an enemy in a declared state of war. The

misunderstanding swelled into a racial conflict between whites and reds that promised to parallel in
its consequences the conflict resulting in the Custer
Battle. That awful massacre, it may be recalled,
had its origin in an event quite as insignificant.

White settlers, scattered among hills and over
plains in little log shacks, blood still curdling at
mention of the Custer fight, were harassed with
terror. Nights they drove their cattle into stock-
ades, double-locked doors, and crawled into bed
fully dressed, guns close at hand, to sleep fitfully
if at all, and dream of ear-splitting whoops and
war paint and bloody scalps. The towns round-
about—Billings, Hardin, Huntley—called for vol-
unteers to form themselves into minute-man or-
ganizations, ready to guard home and family and
town from attack of savage reds. Plea after plea
was sent to Washington for troops. Rumors of an
expected Indian uprising spread throughout the
East. For a time Montana was decidedly, though
unpleasantly, on the map.

Up in Crow, Agent H. E. Williamson was
afraid for his life, a fear not without justification.
Day and night he had a double row of guards stationed round his house. He knew the Indians hated
him; he knew why they hated him, and yet he felt
he was paying too dearly, during this long month
of terror, for his harsh discipline, for those various
acts of his which the Indians were pleased to desig-
nate as treachery and theft.

With the ruthlessness of the bully, with the heedlessness of the man without vision, he had started a ball rolling—a very small harmless ball at first. But it had grown quickly as it rolled along until it was now quite beyond his control and threatened to rebound, undoing all the work of "regenerating" the Indians upon which he had been engaged, robbing him of power and wealth. For his post as Indian Agent appeared to be only a side issue with him. He was also a stockman, rapidly accumulating riches, the vast fertile acres of the Crow grazing land at his disposal.

He joined with the frightened settlers in sending urgent prayers to Mr. Lamar, Secretary of the Interior, for troops to cow the Indians into their accustomed servile obedience. To the agitated plainsmen out in Montana, Washington seemed slow in responding. If so, it was because the matter, according to the unbiased judgment of such men as Lamar and Terry, called for sober consideration. Although only one side, the white man's side, had been presented to them, yet they were convinced that the quarrel must have its two sides.

When Secretary Webb did arrive upon the scene a banquet, sponsored by Mayor Goss of Billings, was tendered in his honor. At that time he said: "Since 1810 the Crows have been the friends of the whites. I do not ever remember reading or hearing of an attack by the Crows against the whites, but, on the contrary, they have always stood by them."

The *Daily Gazette* of October 8, 1887, endeavoring to probe down to the root of the trouble, says this:

"Williamson and Blake offered the government five thousand dollars for grazing permits on part of the Crow reservation. (The last Crow treaty had given the Secretary of the Interior the right to fix the amount for this privilege, and to make leases for the Indians.) This contract between Williamson and Blake and the government was not consummated. Later Williamson wrote the Secretary of the Interior stating that a party of six men, including a certain Briggs, offered twenty thousand dollars for grazing permits on the *remaining* acres of Crow allotment. The government doubtless somewhat mystified by the significance of that word 'remaining' ordered Williamson to lease all or any part of the Crow land to the highest bidder. Williamson replied that 'the Indians would not allow any one on their land except these six men, including Briggs.' No lease was granted the Briggs party but Briggs continued, regardless of Crow protests, to use Crow land for grazing, for which privilege he paid Williamson whatever toll the agent demanded of him."

The *Gazette* adds:

"This affair may have had something to do with the ill-feeling toward Agent Williamson. The Crows talked of putting the matter in the hands of the sheriff, but that is nonsense. *The allotment does not make these Indians citizens nor amenable to civil process.*"

"Agent Williamson," the *Gazette* adds, "is chagrined because his two years' labor among the Indians—regenerating them—goes for nothing. Whatever mistakes the General may have made in his policy, and whatever tendency toward harshness he may have shown (as claimed by some) he must have labored hard to regenerate the Indians."

(Webster defines the word "regenerating": Bringing into a new spiritual life. Making Christians, and so forth. Did Mr. Williamson, we wonder, aim to accomplish this arduous task of regeneration by precept and example?)

It is to be hoped that the years elapsing since 1887 have somewhat tempered our animosity toward our wards and lent generosity and understanding and fair-mindedness to our self-appointed guardianship. To most of those early settlers, however, still embroiled in inherited hatred and fear of the race they had deposed, there was but one side to the question and that was their side.

An editorial in the *Gazette* of October 2, 1887, declares:

"The time for mawkish sentiment is past, and the stern hand of the law should never relax its hold on these Indians until the whole Crow tribe has a wholesome respect for its mandates inculcated into their rebellious hearts."

But, in that same issue, we are rather naively informed:

"A party of Crows were out hunting in the Big Horn Mountains (their own land alloted them by the government) and were pounced upon by a party of whites supposed to be officers from Wyoming Territory who seized their arms, horses, and ammunition, arrested them and marched them to jail."

Concerning that affair the editor refrains from remarking, and nothing, of course, was done. "The Indians were not citizens nor amenable to civil processes."

Group of Crow leaders with interpreters upon their return from Washington where the treaty of 1879 was signed. Photograph by Huffman.

The ball of insurrection, set in motion by Williamson's unwitting hand, rolled on and on, gathering momentum, adding to itself stratum after
stratum of misunderstanding, confusion, bitterness,
fear, hatred, and death. In direct proportion the
agitation of the white settlers, so pitifully alone, so
helpless in their frail shacks in the awfulness of
Montana's vast plains increased. The rumor spread
that a large band of Crows under the leadership of
a young brave known as "Sword-bearer," was for-
tifying itself up in the Big Horn Mountains with
enough food and ammunition to last a year. It
was also rumored that the Blackfeet and the Sioux,
mortal enemies of the Crows but far more bitter
enemies of the whites, were to join the Crows in
one last stand against the common invaders of their
land. Twenty thousand Indians, armed and pro-
visioned, could, unless Washington acted promptly,
wipe the whole of Montana clean of palefaces. A
red terror threatened the peace and happiness, the
very lives, of the white settlers of the Far West,
erstwhile the hunting ground of Indians.

We gather that more and more, during that
time of turmoil, the troubled minds of both the
whites and the peace-inclined Crows were turning
to Plenty Coups. Assuredly Plenty Coups would
be able to talk sense into the hot heads of the rebels
under Sword-bearer. Unfortunately, however,
Plenty Coups could not, at the crucial moment,
be found.

General Terry, forwarding dispatches concerning the Crow insurrection to Washington, said: "I find it difficult to understand this action of the Crows, as they have always been well-behaved and well-disposed, except in respect to feuds with other tribes. In our Sioux trouble they were our faithful and efficient allies. I fear there may be some cause for present excitement, not disclosed by foregoing dispatches. It is surmised the trouble arose from an attempt by the agent to prevent the Indians from having their dance when they were in a state of frenzy following their victorious campaign against their old-time enemy the Piegans (Blackfeet)."

But General Dudley, commandant at Fort Custer, though sincerely desirous of being just, was quite lacking in sympathy for the hostile Indians, and therefore not in accord with General Terry.

So far removed from the seat of trouble it was impossible for Washington to put her finger on the throbbing pulse of controversy and to diagnose properly the swelling abcess of discord. Each day brought from men out in Montana—from Dudley, Williamson, Terry—conflicting reports.

As a result of all this confusion Special Agent Armstrong was sent out to investigate. Armstrong conferred with Williamson and thereafter saw things exactly as that gentleman desired him to see them.

In the *Daily Gazette* for October 7, we read:

"Sword-bearer has under him one hundred and fifty young bucks. The Crows from all over the reservation are coming into the agency, bringing their families with them, begging protection." (The Crows, at this time, were having troubles of their own. They were quite as fearful of an attack by the Piegans as the whites were of an attack by the Crows.)

"Oct. 8—Intense excitement . . . some alarm. Sword-bearer continues hostile. Band of followers increases."

"Oct. 8—Fort Custer—Ration day passed quietly."

"Oct. 14—Fort Custer—Sword-bearer and his party camped on Little Horn forty miles south of Post."

"Oct. 17—Billings—General Sheridan started west to investigate the wide-spread trouble among Indians. Discontent possibly caused by allotment of land in severalty."

"Oct. 17—Fort Custer—Sword-bearer has come down from the mountains where he has been fasting and making medicine."

"October 22—Billings—Sword-bearer and his party have been down to Cheyenne agency inciting insurrection and returned yesterday with recruits."

"Oct. 26—Fort Custer—Two companies of infantry arrived tonight from Ft. Keogh by way of Cheyenne, one of cavalry from Ft. McGinnis, and two from Ft. McKinney. Sword-bearer and party are encamped at 40-mile ranch, close to Custer Battleground. No such preparations for war have been made since 1876. General Dudley will be in command."

"October 27—Billings—Pretty Eagle says that large numbers of the Crow tribe will go to help Sword-bearer if he is arrested. Even well-disposed Indians say there is no doubt but that Sword-bearer possesses occult powers derived from supernatural sources. He predicts and his predictions come true."

"Nov. 2—Billings—Messengers have been sent out to call in all the Crows to the agency. It is hoped they will come peacefully. If they should not Plenty Coups will probably be sent out to influence them to come in."

"Nov. 4—Fort Custer—Seven troops of cavalry left after Sword-bearer. Will have them surrounded by night. The Indians are all at the agency except Plenty Coups. It is hoped he will be there by Sunday."

"Nov. 4—Crow Agency—Two thousand Indians are now here. Sword-bearer and following with them. Arrests will be made on arrival of Plenty Coups."

The editor of the *Gazette* became highly incensed over the turmoil.

"No other course lies open," he writes, "on the part of Agent Armstrong but a vigorous action—even at the cost of life—to teach the Indians the plain fact that they have got to submit to the whites. Disturbances among them, like summer storms, will come and go, leaving a clearer understanding that to become like a white man is their only hope to escape utter annihilation."

A rather paradoxical statement in view of the fact that the whole trouble developed because the young Crow agitator, Sword-bearer, had become very like the white man in his political shrewdness, his vanity and ambition and greed.

Extremely influential among the restless idle young bucks of the Crow tribe was this youth of twenty-four, half Bannock and half Crow, known to the Indians as Chees-ta-pah (He-Who-Wraps-up-His-Tail). He was endowed with a shrewd intellect, a dominating and charming personality, gluttonous thirst for power and a rare gift for leadership. For long, with sullen rage, this attractive young rascal had been noting the growing ascendency of the quiet-mannered, strong-faced, steady-eyed warrior, Plenty Coups. More and more it was Plenty Coups to whom the old chief Pretty Eagle turned for advice in council meetings. Even the whites were conferring with him in matters of weight. Sword-bearer sensed uneasily that Plenty Coups, without apparent effort, was forging ahead toward chieftainship of the entire tribe. And to be made chief of his tribe was the one thing Chees-ta-pah himself desired.

Pretty Eagle was an old man. Soon he must die. Then another chief would be chosen by the Crows. All eyes were turning to Plenty Coups who had made many coups—more, some said, than his friendly rival, Bell Rock—and had proved himself a wise and valiant leader of men. But was not Chees-ta-pah also wise and brave? He lay awake nights, thinking, scheming. He went up into the mountains alone, not, as he would have had his simple followers believe, to pray, but to concoct extravagant campaigns. He possessed all the qualifications of the agitator, youth, rash courage, eloquence, ambition, and, for a time, luck. He could burrow deep into the minds of men, find their peculiar weaknesses, and prey upon them.

Like all agitators, of all times, everywhere, he acquired a following, heady youths, mostly, writhing under the pressure of the white man's foot upon their necks. But, like most agitators, this modern Achilles bungled at the high pinnacle of success and brought disaster down upon himself and his disciples.

Early in the summer of 1887 Chees-ta-pah had somehow come into possession of a cavalry sword, doubtless a gruesome souvenir of the Custer Battle. To the young bucks ever at his heels he made a grandiloquent speech: "This sword," he said, brandishing the bright steel blade over his head, "was sent me by the Great Spirit. Once while I was on the mountain top making strong medicine it came floating down to me from the Blue. While I carry it nothing can harm me or any of my followers—no poisoned arrow—no white man's bullets."

His gullible audience, fascinated and intoxicated by his youthful charm, his undeniable eloquence, the nameless something which drew and held men, believed him. Was he not a favorite child of the Great Spirit and had not the Great Spirit bestowed supernatural powers upon him? Thenceforth he became known as "Sword-bearer." And for a time luck helped him play his hand. A series of coincidences, rather remarkable, added testimony to his brazen assertions.

Possessed of something more than ordinary ability in diagnosing weather conditions he prophesied a storm, and lo, after a day or two it did storm!

Then, one day while he and his band of bucks were on a raiding party, a thunder storm came up. A dart of lightning zigzagged across the sky, killing a few cattle. Sword-bearer was quick to utilize the situation. He flourished his charmed sword and shouted: "It was I, Sword-bearer, who brought the stream of fire down from the Blue. Thus, whenever I hold my sword aloft and speak certain words, fire descends and kills my enemies."

Later, when the white man's cannon from Fort Custer was aimed at his group of faithful ones, he importuned them not to fear.

"The gun of the white man cannot harm us," he cried. "Look! I hold my sword aloft and speak and the gun shall be destroyed."

And again luck was with the clever liar. The gun, after the one shot that went over their heads, became disabled and could not be used for weeks. The recoil had burst the fastenings and, before the very eyes of the credulous, awed Indians, it was dismounted. Sword-bearer had proved himself invincible indeed. To deny him was to deny the Great Spirit.

Even wise old Pretty Eagle said to General Armstrong: "The Crows do not want to fight the whites but are afraid of the medicine man who says that unless we join him he will destroy us all. And he is a great man. All things bend before him. The very ground is now shaking before he does his great deeds."

A harrowing time, that fall of 1887, for both the Crows and the whites. Sword-bearer alone was happy, riding gay and triumphant on the very crest of the wave of power.

This was the sort of man the Crows needed

now, so argued the hot-headed boys, this great
medicine man, Sword-bearer, who could control
with a word the heavens and the earth, and who
could render impotent the belching fire-machines
of the whites. Here was a mighty leader, most certainly sent straight down from the Blue just when
they were threatened with tribal effacement, to
restore to them their vast hunting grounds and their
old joyous existence and their liberty. Day by day
his popularity waxed and his string of proselytes
lengthened.

Recently Blackfeet had stolen horses from the
Crows. That act was a tribal insult, a flagrant
declaration of war. To ignore it would stamp upon the Crows forever the brand of cowardice. It
placed them in much the situation America faced
when the *Lusitania* was sunk. So, inspired by patriotism and pricked by ambition and vanity and
the audacious spirit of youth, Sword-bearer and
his men set out early one morning in the summer
of 1887 to raid the Blackfeet and recover the stolen
horses. They left Crow village that morning, all
bedecked with eagle feathers, sitting their horses
proudly, making a gay splash of color against the
sun-bronzed plains.

Returning a few days later they drove ahead of
them not only their own horses but also several belonging to the enemy. Sword-bearer had taken a
picketed horse; he had made coup; he was a brave
warrior; he was wild with joy. Approaching Crow

village he let out one lusty whoop after another
and quirted his horse on to a gallop, for he wished
to make a spectacular entrance into town and receive the acclamation of his people.

He was young. He was elated into madness by
his victory. His followers caught the contagion of
his enthusiasm and added their whoops to his.
Thundering into Crow, the triumphant braves
dashed up and down quiet streets, yelling, shooting
into the air. They circled the house of Government
Agent Williamson, perhaps, with young conceit,
incited to "show off" before the pompous agent
whom they all so heartily detested. All at once the
serenity of the somnolent village was shattered by
a riot of savage yells and shots and the thunder of
galloping hoofs.

A man acquainted with tribal customs and who
understood the Indians and sympathized with them
—such a man as Terry—would have made nothing
of the occurrence. But Williamson came plunging
into the melee, startled, indignant. One of the wild
shots sang past his head, doubtless too close for the
equanimity of that gentleman's nerves. Instantly
he was enraged, and ordered the braves arrested for
horse-stealing. The bewildered young leader who
had anticipated a warm welcome with feasting and
dancing found himself in unaccountable disgrace.

Passionately those Indians resented the seeming
injustice of arrest. According to their ethics of
warfare they had conducted themselves admirably.

They were not horse thieves; they were warriors. Having invaded the enemy's camp and fought a successful battle they had returned with booty.

Wisdom, tact, kindness, at that crucial moment might have written a happier page in the history of Crows and whites. But Williamson lacked wisdom. He was neither tactful nor kind. These hot-headed savages had stolen horses and had shot at him. They must be punished. He meant to teach them a lesson they wouldn't soon forget, to teach them "the plain fact that they have got to submit to the whites, that to become like a white man is their only hope to escape from utter annihilation."

Unfortunately he ignored completely their tribal traditions, their intense pride, their fierce loyalty to their own. He fanned into quick flame the vindictive hatred toward himself which for long had been smoldering in the hearts of all of them.

However, before his orders could be carried out, the outraged Sword-bearer and his insurgents fled up into the mountains. Up to that moment, presumably, Sword-bearer had entertained no notion of warring against the whites, his ambition having been limited to chieftainship of his tribe. But he was quick to grasp the possibilities of the situation thrust upon him. He saw visions—another battle against the palefaces such as the Sioux had waged so successfully at Custer—the whites defeated—all the buffalo plains of the Crows restored to them—

and he, the mighty Sword-bearer, their honored chief, greatest warrior of all time. The fever of glory, scented from afar, ran hot in his veins.

Stealthily at night he traveled down into the Crow reserve, returning each time with added satellites. His band swelled into some three hundred young bucks, easy victims of the eloquence of the magnetic leader. With shrewd forethought and meticulous care Sword-bearer mapped out his campaign. He pulled every available wire. He visited the Sioux and so charmed those lifelong enemies of the Crows with his affable social graces and his dancing that when he returned to his mountain retreat recruits from the Sioux village went trailing along behind. A visit to the Blackfeet was not less fruitful.

This gave foundation for the rumor rapidly spreading through the terrified white settlement down in the valley that the Sioux tribes and the Blackfeet were joining forces with the Crows to exterminate the palefaces.

Success intoxicated Sword-bearer. Often during those glamorous days of his insurgency he leaped upon a rock, a dominating personage against the background of grim mountains, and harangued his subjects. He reminded them, in words that scorched down to their very souls, of the wrongs they had endured under the rule of invading whites.

"Once," he shouted, brandishing his bright sword so that it glittered in the sunlight, "once all this beautiful land from the Rockies where the sun sets to the Father of Waters where it rises belonged to the red man. Then he was free and he was happy. Then his stomach and the stomachs of his squaws and papooses were always filled with fat buffalo meat. Then he might go where he wished, do as he wished. Now palefaces say to us—to us, lords of the plains, mighty warriors, they say: 'This much land you may have and no more.' They dare to give us a small part of our own. And we are fed like slaves—like dogs—from the locked storehouses of the agents. We *are* slaves. Many times when I have been up in the mountains seeking visions our forefathers have come down to me from the Blue and have spoken to me.

" 'You, young Crows and Blackfeet and Sioux of today, you are squaw-hearted. Palefaces have taken from you the land for which your fathers fought and you have done nothing. They have slaughtered your buffalo and now you are without meat for food or hides for clothing or tepees. You, Sword-bearer, have been sent by us to our people to lead them to freedom and to restore their past glory.'

"Such words did our forefathers speak to me up on mountain tops. Now we shall no longer be squaw-hearted. We will fight. We will win. We will recover the land which the Great Spirit gave to His children the red men, to be theirs forever. I have spoken."

While Sword-bearer and his warriors were encamped at Rotten Grass, old Chief Pretty Eagle,
worn with weight of anxiety, visited them and endeavored to persuade them to return and submit
to arrest.

"It is true," he told them, "that we have been
unjustly treated and that our land has been taken
from us. The Great Spirit has shown that He loves
His white children best. Now we must yield, not
because we are cowards, but because we are wise.
If you, hiding in the mountains, fight against the
palefaces you will fail. Then, not only yourselves
but all the Crows and Sioux and Blackfeet will be
punished. The whites will fight until not one red
man is left on the plains. It is true we are slaves
but, if we are obedient slaves, we shall escape much
suffering. If we rebel the cannon of the White
Father will scatter us as wind scatters dried leaves.
His great cannon will bark and we will be wiped
away."

Instantly Sword-bearer sprang up in front of
Pretty Eagle, waving his gleaming sword. "Paleface cannon will not hurt us," he cried. "With my
sword I will destroy the cannon and cause it to
cease belching forth fire and death."

The old chief sighed. "Sword-bearer," he said,
wearily, "speaks with crooked tongue."

"They call us 'thieves,'" Sword-bearer shouted.
"They, the palefaces, who make treaties only to
break them, who have stolen our buffalo and our
land, they call us 'thieves.'"

With a gesture Pretty Eagle arrested the other's wild flow of words. "The day of the red man," he said gravely, "is past. The day of the white man is here. My day, too, is past. I am old. My young men no longer heed my words. I will send Plenty Coups to speak words of wisdom to you."

But Plenty Coups was not at his lodge. He was not at Pryor. He could not be found.

Bill Hamilton rode up from Billings to talk things over with Pretty Eagle. "You Crows," he said, "have always been friends and allies of the whites. We don't want to fight you but we've got to maintain order."

"Sword-bearer," Pretty Eagle said, "will not submit to arrest when he has done no wrong."

" 'Not done wrong!' Why, out here we hang horse thieves!"

"Blackfeet take our horses," the chief explained patiently. "We take their horses. That is war."

Hamilton nodded. "I understand," he said. "But you can't make Williamson or Dudley or Armstrong understand. Do you know troops are coming from Fort Keogh and McGinnis to force the Crows to submission?"

"Yes," said Pretty Eagle, sadly, "I know."

"Well, why don't you send Plenty Coups up to reason with Sword-bearer? He might make the scalawags come to time."

"We cannot find Plenty Coups," Pretty Eagle admitted.

Hamilton frowned thoughtfully. "Funny!" he muttered. "I'll go home through Pryor Pass. If I find him I'll send him to you."

Meanwhile, at command of General Dudley, Pretty Eagle had dispatched runners through Big Horn and Pryor Valley, calling his people in. Many, afraid of raiding Piegans, were already camped close to Crow. The rest came hurrying in, each buck with his family and tepee and horses and dogs. They were terrified. They set tepees close together, each finding comfort in the proximity of the other, or else dug holes far back into hillsides where they could crawl, at a moment's notice, away from barking cannon. They were quite as afraid of the whites as the whites, sleeping behind barred doors, guns at hand, down in Billings, were of them.

What was to be the end? Day after day, hour after hour, the Indians waited in anguished uncertainty, with that mute patience tribulation had taught them, for something to happen. And constantly their eyes turned toward the Pryor Mountains. Now, when they were facing the greatest crisis of their tribal existence, why did not Plenty Coups hasten to his people? They needed his strength, his faith, his calm far-seeing wisdom.

Sword-bearer's little day was almost ended. Up on Rotten Grass, though he steadfastly resisted arrest and continued to spout courage to his followers, yet, hourly, more and more of his bravado was being squeezed out of his tortured soul. Like many another young agitator he found himself in a quandary. He knew that against the troops he and his men could not hold out. If he did not surrender and if they captured him alive he would be shackled and locked in the white man's jail, the extremest indignity that mind of Indian can fancy. There might, too, because of him, be suffering and blood-shed among his people. But, on the other hand, to surrender now after all his loud vaunts of super-natural power would make of him the laughing stock of his whole tribe. And to an Indian ridicule is torture.

He knew not what to do, which way to turn. After all, Sword-bearer was but twenty-four years old, a zealous patriot despite ambition and vanity and foolhardiness, and his blackest crime hitherto had been the looting of enemy plunder.

Finally, one long moon since the momentous morning when, jubilant over his victory, he had ridden madly about the streets of Crow, he and his followers skulked down from the mountain and camped in the brush on the banks of Little Horn. There, still stubborn, defiant, frightened, vindic-tive, he waited action of the soldiers. And Dudley delayed action day after day, waiting the arrival of Plenty Coups.

From the *Daily Gazette*:

"Crow Agency, Nov. 3, 1887—Two thousand Indians are now here (in Crow). Sword-bearer and his following with them. Arrests will be made on the arrival of Plenty Coups. All Indians now in camp except Plenty Coups and his band on Pryor."

The strain of waiting was showing on the faces of the terrorized Crows. Sword-bearer, still at liberty but under constant surveillance, bore little resemblance to the haughty young demigod of a month ago. His sunken eyes, in a gaunt, worn face, were wild with the agony of suspense. And hour after hour runners sent out in search of Plenty Coups returned despondent.

Daily Gazette:

"Billings, Nov. 5, 1887—Early this morning a council of headmen of the Crows was held. Pretty Eagle acted as spokesman. General Armstrong told them that some of them had been bad. He said Pretty Eagle must give up these bad ones to the soldiers. Pretty Eagle said he would give up Sword-bearer but not the others."

During the council meeting Hamilton dashed into Crow, horse stumbling with fatigue, and shouted: "I've found Plenty Coups."

A dozen anxious voices demanded: "Where? Is he coming? When will he be here?"

"Plenty Coups will be here tomorrow," Hamilton assured them.

"Where has he been all this time?"

"James Campbell found him," Hamilton said. "Plenty Coups says to tell you, the Crows, and you, the white brothers, that he does not sympathize with the bad Indian."

Gazette:

"Crow Agency. Nov. 5, 1887—Several tragic incidents occurred today. One Indian was covered by a six-shooter in the hands of a soldier and called upon to surrender, and before he could be stopped he pulled his gun and shot himself."

"Fort Custer. Nov. 5, Dispatch to Mayor Goss—Fight this afternoon. Sword-bearer and two Indians killed. One corporal killed and two soldiers wounded. Balance of Indians captured. No cause for alarm.

Signed. (Sec.) WM. B. WEBB."

"Fort Custer, Nov. 5, 11:20 p. m. (To A. Fraser.) All right. No need for alarm. Sword-bearer and three Indians killed. One soldier killed, two wounded. No danger now.

Signed. A. H. HERSEY."

"Crow Agency. Nov. 7 (to Walter Cooper). Your workmen need fear no trouble with the Crows.

Signed. THOS. H. RUGER. (Brig. Gen.)"

Billings *Gazette:*

"Nov. 7, 1887—Plenty Coups arrived day before yesterday ahead of his people, who got in yesterday. He would have been here before but was found by James Campbell away from home, up in the mountains, mourning his loss. His wife (Flying Bird) died last week. Plenty Coups says he is very sorry trouble occurred and that if he had been here he thought it might have been prevented. He says everything is going to be all right now."

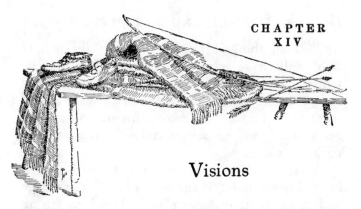

Visions

WHEN A-Leek-Chea-Ahoosh was sixteen years old it came time for him to go up onto the mountain and see visions and receive his strong medicine. So one morning in early spring he went down to the creek, broke the thin scum of ice, and bathed in the chilled waters. Then he started out alone across the plains toward the mountains, headed for the deepest spiritual adventure of his life.

Crow Indians have always gone up onto the high places to worship their deity—temples ready built by the Great Spirit for His children. To them the mountain with its awesome silences, its overpowering grandeur, has seemed emblematic of divinity, a God-made altar. They may have believed that its peak reached up into the very heart of the spirit land.

After many snows had fallen upon the head of A-Leek-Chea-Ahoosh and he became an old man, known to the world as Chief Plenty Coups, he had occasion to speak before a large assembly of Indians and white men.

"Of all things created," he said, "the mountains only have escaped the domination of the white man. The valleys are scarred by the plow man, ridged by the trail maker and guttered by the taker of water, but the mountains are still as God made them, and to be near them is to be on the pathway to peace."

That same ardent love for the mountains burned in the heart of the boy as he left the village and trudged across the plains. His lean strong young body was stripped naked save for breech cloth and moccasins. Although he would journey many sleeps he carried with him neither food nor water. He went out from his mother's tepee a boy. When he returned—if he did return—he would have become a man.

By the time the sun was high in the Blue he had reached the base of the mountain. All that day he climbed upward and steadily upward, circling deep cañons, scrambling over fallen logs and boulders—the accumulated debris of centuries—working his way inch by inch up steep rocky precipices, clinging with fingers and toes.

From time to time he looked down from his dizzy height and across the plains to the village of his people. At first he could see men moving about and children and horses and dogs. Faint thin sounds of life came seeping up to him through the distance. Then, each time he looked, the camp grew smaller, became blurred, until it was a mere dark blotch against the plains. And then he rounded a boulder and lost sight of it altogether.

Night was approaching. The sun had slipped back of a high peak and was painting long soft purple shadows of the mountains upon the plains. To the boy it seemed very cold, very dark, very still, so high up against the Blue. He was weary and hungry; already the torment of thirst had begun to assail him. But, more than all else, he was afraid—dreadfully afraid—of the still loneliness of that awful solitude into which he was plunging. The heavy dark settling all about him he knew to be peopled with evil spirits. Voices came out of the dark, the mournful swish of pine trees, the long-drawn-out howl of a coyote, the tinkle of a loose stone rattling down—down. He lay close to a tree and huddled there, wide-open eyes staring into the night, ears strained, nerves taut.

In fancy he pictured the warm, cozy, lighted security of his mother's tepee and yearned for it, unspeakably. Yet he entertained no thought of retreat, for he was searching for his God who would surely come to him somewhere up in the Blue.

Visions — Buddha — Strong Medicine — Mohammed—Great Spirit— "What matter how you name God or in what words you praise Him?" It matters only that in the soul of man be found the essence of religion.

There was spiritual beauty within the soul of the savage red man who, in his perplexities, his desperate need, his thirst for truth, sought his God in visions on the mountain top.

All of the first night A-Leek-Chea-Ahoosh lay in a pine thicket, sheltering his naked body as best he could from winds that swept bitingly over the heights. When morning came he continued his climb, though more slowly, for his moccasins had worn thin and he was weary and footsore. By the end of the second day he had reached the very peak of the mountain. There he must remain, the hot sun beating down upon him by day and chill winds sweeping over him by night, until hunger and thirst and exhaustion induced fever and delirium and visions came to him.

But the boy would not recognize his excited condition as delirium. He would become light-headed and giddy. The torments of thirst would madden him. He would drift off into unconsciousness and then he would be visited by that which was to guard and guide him all through life. For him the experience would be exalted, spiritual, mystic.

A-Leek-Chea-Ahoosh lay down on a rock on the topmost peak of the mountain. He was beyond all physical suffering, he felt nothing. He had climbed very close to the mysterious Blue, so close that there was nothing between him and it. Between him and the world of men down below floated clouds that isolated him in a strange silent solitude, vast, complete, stupendous. And presently there came to him the eagle or the vision of the eagle that was to be his strong medicine, and he received spiritual baptism.

"Where there is no vision the people perish." The Crow Indian has fold upon fold of superstition enwrapping his religion, but strip it bare, clean down to the fundamental truth, and we find the constituent of all religions, an impulse upward, a quest for that which will fulfill the peculiar needs of the individual, and that in every case, however we name it, is God.

Unquestionably the boy found his God as he lay on the rock high up on the mountain with mists enshrouding him. To hear the old man Plenty Coups relate, solemnly, reverently, that youthful experience is to be convinced of the poignant significance of his soul's adventure up into the Blue.

Some ages ago a man named Moses went up onto a mountain. "And the glory of the Lord abode upon Mt. Sinai, and the cloud covered it six days and the seventh day He called unto Moses out of the midst of the cloud." Plenty Coups says, with profound faith: "And I was up there so long alone I thought I was going to die, and then an eagle came to me, and straight down from the Blue, a white man. Then I knew I would live long and be happy." The Lord, we cannot doubt, called also unto Plenty Coups out of the midst of the cloud.

Great heights, vast distances, solitude, meditation, implicit faith in a higher power, life after death, those things composed the Crow Indian's religion, a religion that sufficed for the ethical needs of his existence until the advent of civilization as epitomized by palefaces who began zealously to teach the Indian that "to become like a white man is his only hope to escape utter annihilation." The simple savage was nonplussed to learn that there was only one true God—the white man's God— and only one right way—the white man's way.

But the white man's way was not and never could be his way. This same white man, speaking glibly of brotherly love and a merciful God, invaded the Indian's country and took his lands and destroyed his only means of sustenance. So the white man must have spoken with crooked tongue, for no brother would do to another what the white man has done to the Indian, and no merciful God would permit the desecration of the rights of His children if He loved them.

So they reasoned among themselves, these puzzled pagans. And they continued to climb the mountain for visions and strong medicine. They clung to the religion of their fathers that meant to them beauty and peace and truth.

Little by little, of late, civilization has been loosening the shackles with which she bound her copper-skinned children. Formerly it was decided for them where they should live, what and how

much they should eat, what they should wear—so
many pounds of meat, so many yards of calico, so
many acres of land—an arrangement deemed necessary to protect them from fraud. In this republic
the bare necessities of existence were doled out to
the first American at the discretion of the super-
intendent who classified his wards as "competent"
or "incompetent." Their comfort, their happiness
was, and still is, dependent upon the whim of a
government agent. Sometimes it chances that the
agent is honest and earnest, having at heart only
the best good of the people under his supervision.
Then they fare well and progress. Sometimes he is
a dogmatic overlord, issuing orders through an interpreter, making no attempt even to learn the
Indian's language so he may approach nearer an
understanding of his innermost thoughts and perplexities and aspirations. Often he is a grafter, be-
traying his position of trust, padding his own
pockets while the Indian and his family live in
poverty.

Valentine, in his report as Commissioner for the
year 1911, says: "Indian affairs are, even under the
best possible administration, peculiarly a field for
the grafter. The lands and the money of the Indian offer a bait which the most satiated fish will
not refuse."

It gives us food for thought that almost every
act passed by our government that broadens in the
slightest degree the liberty of the Indian, that

loosens by ever so little the shackles binding him, ends with the vaguely restricting phrase: "In the discretion of the Secretary of the Interior."

And the discretion of the Secretary of the Interior is biased, necessarily, by the report of the agent who is presumably in a position to understand existing conditions on the reservation. His statement is usually accepted as final. Against it the Indian has no appeal.

The civilized white man has deemed it best that his copper-skinned pagan brother, the erstwhile liberty-loving, wild folks of the plains, be farmers —all of them. And so it is decreed. After untold centuries of life under a certain self-prescribed social order they have been thrust willy-nilly into another social order prescribed by an alien and recently inimical race. They have been robbed, among other things, of individual initiative.

Some Indians are naturally agriculturists, but not the Crows. What they might have become if left to their own resources we can never know. We do know that the white man, in his effort to "regenerate" them, has bungled lamentably.

One spring a certain magisterial agent distributed potatoes among his wards with the curt order: "Plant these!" and then, during summer months, dismissed the matter from his mind, complacently convinced that he had done his whole duty.

In the fall, at potato-digging time, he drove through the Crow Reservation from one little log shack to another, but nowhere did he see potato patches.

Finally he inquired of one old squaw: "I gave you potatoes to plant last spring. Where are they? Why didn't they come up?"

The Indian woman shrugged. "Potatoes good in spring," she explained. "Plant 'em. In fall maybe so, good, maybe so, no. Me no plant potatoes. Me eat 'em."

It is a laughable story, of course, but back of the nonsense is logic of a kind, and back of that pathos. The squaw and her children were hungry. The rations allotted them were not enough to satisfy their hunger. No one had taken the pains to explain to her that unalterable law by which potatoes put in the ground are bound to produce more potatoes. The temptation to cook them and eat them rather than bury them where they might, or might not multiply—Maybe so, yes. Maybe so, no —was too strong to be resisted.

Among the Crows are a few successful farmers. It is a matter of history that Plenty Coups, in the years of his prime, exhibited at agricultural fairs the biggest potatoes raised in Yellowstone County. But that was characteristic of the man—to attempt to excel in anything he undertook. Among the Crows, along with a few successful farmers, are also singers, artists, orators, writers, a talented race of folk who might, were they not inhibited by racial timidity—a timidity born of years of suppression and ridicule—achieve a place in the climb toward a cultural life.

Cato Sells, Commissioner, in his report for the year 1915, says: "I repudiate the suggestion that the Indian is a vanishing race. He should march side by side with the white man during all the years that are to come." And he adds: "Do you think it possible to take too seriously a responsibility involving the health, education, property, and, in some cases, the destiny of a human race?"

That we are responsible for their destiny is undeniable. We assumed that responsibility when we took possession of their land, and with it their only means of livelihood, and dictated to them the manner and the place in which they must henceforth live. Whether, left to their own initiative in the whirlagig complexities of the machine age of civilization, they would prove themselves fit to survive is a debatable question. To their former environment which, though less complex, did demand intelligence and courage and endurance, they adapted themselves readily, even built up a system of government socialistic in nature, based upon the creed of brotherly love that had in it no place for graft or crime.

One Commissioner says: "An Indian thrown into contact only with people of his own race cannot satisfactorily develop and broaden. He has only the vaguest comprehension of putting out one dollar today in order to get two dollars tomorrow."

The Commissioner fails to define exactly what he means by "satisfactory development." If he means commercialism, competing against the white man in his insane struggle for dollars, he is presumably right. The word "money" is not found in the original Indian vocabulary. But if by "satisfactory development" he means mental and soul growth, then some few who know the Indian best have dared to hint that he has passed the white man in the race.

Because the average Crow is not a successful farmer the white man refers to him glibly as "lazy." Concerning laziness Morley has this to say: "Few people are really lazy. What we call laziness is merely maladjustment. For, in any department of life where one is generally interested, we will be zealous beyond belief."

If the Crow Indian is, as has often been affirmed, in a state of "economic stagnation," it is, possibly, because of maladjustment. Put him where he wants to be, give him an opportunity to do the thing he wants to do, and he is not lazy. He will not stagnate.

But what does he want to do, where does he want to be? Assuredly not a farmer, back of a plow.

Mr. I. D. O'Donnel, representing the Great Northern as expert agriculturist among the Indians, says: "I have a theory. Whether it is a good one or not remains to be seen. Crow Indians are hunters and fighting men. For countless past ages ambitious Indian boys have fitted themselves for one of two careers: the hunter or the warrior. Their peculiar environment made those two avocations of special importance. Now their environment has changed and with it the demand for hunters and warriors. But the heart of man is not changed over night. To mold the wild young savage riding long adventurous miles across unfenced plains into a farmer, guiding his plow up one furrow and down another is an impossibility. Nor does the notion of killing for food the pig and cow he has raised and to which he has become attached appeal to him. But he loves horses. Instead of compelling him to toil at something distasteful to him why not turn his natural inclinations into assets? Why not make of him a stockman, a sheepman, a cattleman or a breeder of fine horses? Then he could ride his horse and spend his time from daylight till dark on the plains."

Formerly the highest goal conceived by Indian mind was chieftainship of his tribe, a position demanding shrewdness, military skill, caution, judgment, patience, courage, all those qualities that go to the making of an executive. Now, with those same qualities still dormant within him, he is heading toward racial oblivion. The swift current of civilization is bearing him onward, with every second his frail craft of individualism threatened by monstrous ships of commercialism.

The question assails us: Why has a race of people admittedly fine, intelligent, ambitious, energetic, talented, remained dormant when for the past five hundred years it has been in close contact with a people of supposedly superior culture?

Dr. Marquis, who has written many books on Indian life, maintains that it is a question whether the Indian is a step behind the white man in cultural development.

"Am I above their level of intelligence?" he queried. "I doubt it. I can pound the typewriter. I can come somewhat nearer expressing my thoughts in words than they, but then, they can do things I can't do. Crow children are showing a more marked aptitude—mind you, I say 'aptitude' —for music and painting than a corresponding number of white children. As physician and writer and friend I have been so fortunate as to associate with Indians intimately for years. Among them are many fine men and women. I feel that I am stronger, broader, better, for my contact with them. But I do not know them. I don't think any paleface can boast that he really knows an Indian."

The blanket or the dress suit, moccasins or leather shoes, tepee or house, long braids or hair cut short. We suffer from tribal egotism, we human beings. We each think our tribe vastly superior to any other tribe. We are inclined to set up a mold, and whatever tribe fails, in color, habits, morals, to pour itself into that mold, is, necessarily, inferior to us. We are invariably right and the rest of the universe is therefore wrong.

Perhaps to the Indian the path of peace he has been following seems more desirable than the white man's crowded road toward material prosperity.

So alien is the small group of red men to the civilization enwrapping it that it would seem they must be crushed by its folds until we recall that they still have their visions, without which a people perish.

One Sunday morning in October of 1931, whites from Red Lodge and Hardin and Billings drove up to Lodge Grass to attend Crow religious services. We passed through the little tree-shaded village of Crow and on over the trail Custer and his men had followed to their death fifty-four years ago. On the rims to the right of us were the ruins of old Fort Custer, to the left a hill dotted with white stones marking the last stand of Custer's men. In this valley of the Big Horn, where so many of life's dramas have been staged, half a century ago young Doc Bill Allen met Plenty Coups for the first time and shared with him a buffalo feast. Here, on the banks of the Little Horn, the ambitious, vainglorious young patriot, Sword-bearer, defied the whites and met death. Through this same valley the lad, A-Leek-Chea-Ahoosh, led his first war party in a raid against the Sioux and recaptured the Crows' stolen horses and made coup. Was all the valley, we wondered, garish with au-

Home of Chief Plenty Coups. Photograph by Ruth Ann Hines.
See page 276.

tumn tints that fall morning sixty-five years ago
as the Crow boy rode along, singing his war songs
and thinking his love thoughts, young heart aflame
with the thrill of his big adventure, all of life
before him?

He was not at church this Sunday morning.
Plenty Coups is an old man; his sight is dim; visions
come to him now from within; his path of peace
must lead him shortly to the Happy Hunting
Ground.

Perhaps the drive through the historic valley,
splashed with crimson and gold and russet and
emerald and silver, had mesmerized us by its
beauty, but it did seem, as we entered the little
church where Crows, of late, have worshipped,
that a peace settled upon us, such a peace as pass-
ing years are wont to destroy.

The whites were seated on one side of the
church, the Indians on the other, with nothing to
separate us but a narrow aisle, drawn very close
after dark years of racial misunderstanding and
hatred, by a singleness of purpose, a search for
truth.

Reverend Petzol, for eighteen years pastor of
the Crow church at Lodge Grass, welcomed us.

"You never know the people of another
tongue," he said, "until you see their approach to
their deity. I have worked with the Crow people
for eighteen years. I think they are the finest racial
group in all the earth. There is no people anywhere

that has been so experimented with as these people. Every government agent who comes sweeps away all that has been done before and starts over again."

While he spoke I studied the dark faces across the aisle. Thoughtful they were and earnest, beautiful with a sublime serenity one does not often find on the tense, harassed faces of whites.

White Arm led in prayer. He stood up before us, a large, rugged-faced, middle-aged Indian, wearing dark glasses, and, with hand upraised, prayed to his God and ours in Crow.

Fred, another Indian, spoke to us, Robert Yellow-tail interpreting. Fred said: "We have all met here this beautiful Sunday morning, worshippers in the true sense of God Almighty. We, his children, have met here in brotherhood to shake each other's hands. It took me some time to realize that this way of living is the right way. I realize now that the long delayed move should have been made long ago. Those that follow Christ have something to be thankful for every day of their lives. I am glad to gather together and look into the faces of the white people who believe as we believe."

Following his speech a double quartet of young Crow men and women sang "Child of Sorrow and of Woe." Their voices blended and rose, clear and sweet and true. They have, indeed, for the past five hundred years, been children of sorrow and of woe, confronted by problems that have vexed few racial groups.

Next a Crow spoke to us haltingly, earnestly, in broken English: "I have gone through lots of hard times," he said, "but there is nothing that has caressed my spirit like the assurance of God's love and care. I am talking to an audience as how probably knows more about God than I do in my humble way. But I am glad they have come here to see that we are trying to know God as they do."

Following a solo by a Crow girl, Alice Frost, in a contralto voice, hauntingly sweet, John Whiteman spoke.

"First," he said, "you must excuse my broken English. You know how it is. I am a full-blood Crow. The Lord made me first to speak the Crow language.

"Whatever our racial creed we must worship the one God. We Crows are trying to find our places in the sun. We are developing the church. The church board is made up of Indian men. We have voted toward the church budget $800 for this year. It is a big reach for us but we are trying to make it. We have Bible school, prayer-meeting and an Indian choir.

"We like to be forward-looking people and forge ahead. We interpret your presence here today as a sign of your friendship and your interest in our effort to better our condition."

How humble they are, these simple, groping Crows, in face of the arrogant assumption that the whites and their ways are always right!

They have been experimented with time after time, in kindliness and in arrogance. Agents have come to them, sent from the White Father, have molded their lives and attempted to mold their souls, as though they were made of putty. Agent follows agent. Each has taken that putty, fashioned according to some vague idea of his predecessor, and has smoothed and patted and begun remolding. No one seems to remember that God made man in His own image, that the soul of the Indian, along with the soul of the white man, was molded on that sixth day of Creation and that God saw everything He had made and pronounced it good.

Some seventy years ago the boy A-Leek-Chea-Ahoosh went up onto the mountain, into the majesty of vast still distances, seeking his deity, and he called that deity "Strong Medicine." Today the Indian boy seeks Him in a man-made temple and calls his deity "God." In the heart of each is the same impulse to seek upward for truth. To each have come visions.

So long as a people have visions, so long shall they prove themselves strong to combat racial prejudices and survive.

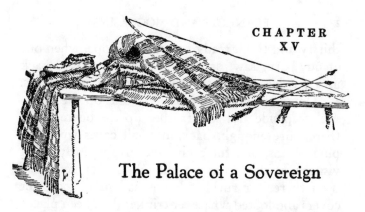

The Palace of a Sovereign

ONE SUNDAY morning in early September of
1931, the day before the opening of the "Midland Empire Fair," we drove up to Pryor to visit
Chief Plenty Coups. A trip to the Pryor Mountains meant an escape from the sweltering heat we
had been enduring for weeks. It meant a heaven
of sparkling streams and pine-spiced air and miles
and miles of vivid green, fringing creeks and car-
peting slopes.

Our road wound out and up into russet-brown
hills dabbed here and there with the bright emerald
of soap weed—brave things that defy hot rainless
summers. Some ten miles out from Billings we
parked our car and tramped across coulees and up
and down buttes searching for old Indian graves
that rumor had told us were somewhere about.
Time after time we had explored that region un-
successfully, but this morning luck favored us.
After an hour of fruitless search over hills radiating
unbearable heat, we stood on a point, hot and

thirsty and tired, ready to abandon hope, when one of our party saw, or thought he saw, shoved back into crevices across the coulee, several pine boxes.

Down the coulee we plunged and up the opposite steep side and still farther up the butte. And there, sure enough, back in small caves were five pine coffins, one for each cave. Apparently other visitors, as curious as we, though less reverent, had been there, for ruthless hands had pried loose the covers and looted whatever trinkets had been placed beside the dead. We saw only skeletons, fragments of buckskin clothing, and wisps of long coarse black hair.

In one smaller box placed at the head of a larger one were tiny baby bones, and brightly tinted ashes that puzzled us until we discovered hanging to a crag a few feet below the coffin, a gaudy Indian blanket that crumbled at our touch into the same red ashes.

Near the group a rude wooden cross had been fixed into the ground, but with no inscription upon it. Who the Indians were, what caused their death, how long they had reposed there, probably no one will ever learn. If the Crows know they will not tell, for Indians do not willingly speak of their sacred dead. To do so endangers the peace of soul of the departed, may even recall them from the Happy Hunting Ground to wander desolated upon earth.

But what does it matter? That mass of

bleached bones seemed scarcely gruesome to us, so little did it suggest that which makes man—hopes, ambitions, fears, despair, love, hate, grief. Just bones; doubtless the hands that had placed them there, lovingly, prayerfully, had also long since turned to ashes. A fitting mausoleum in which to sleep the last sleep—the hushed quiet of the hills brooding over them, the pines singing their eternal anthem to them.

Returning to our car we followed the road that cut a twisting gash through the hills, barren, brown, lifeless hills, rolling on and on to the mountains. Presently we left the main highway, taking a trail that led to the west, and almost instantly the landscape changed. We were entering mountain country—Crow country—and drew long breaths of pungent, tonic air coming down from snow-capped peaks that dispersed lethargy and charged us with joyous energy. Here hills were green and cattle browsed upon them and vagrant little streams sprang from nowhere and went trickling down to nowhere.

In another half hour we had reached the Indian village of Pryor, a sleepy town with a cluster of log cabins and a store or two nestling at the foot of the mountains. Fifty years ago, in the days of his prime, Plenty Coups had, among his various activities, run a store here successfully. But now it seemed that the god of indolence had pressed a hand heavily upon the place. Save for a lazy dog sprawled in the thick dust of the street, we saw no living thing.

Indeed, over all that wide green valley of Pryor with its cottonwood groves and its streams there hovers always an ineffable beauty of peace—a startling absence of the buzz and clamor of existence—that is balm to frazzled nerves. One wonders if such peace does not account in a measure for the remarkable serenity of expression on the faces of the Indians who live there.

Plenty Coups' dwelling is a log house about three miles out of Pryor back from the road in a grove of cottonwoods. As we drove up the lane and approached the rambling old house in its setting of cool dark shadows, I admit that I was deeply moved. This was the home of a great and famous man, the ruler of a people, an avowed sovereign. I had heard much of him and now I was about to speak to him, and, if he proved gracious, hear him speak.

That he has been a wise ruler, leading his subjects through hectic years of disturbance and readjustment, still holding their respect, their reverence and loyalty, none can doubt. Not every monarch, after fifty years' stormy reign, can boast as much. The homage that one vouchsafes freely to genuine worth was in our hearts as we rapped at his door. But Plenty Coups was not at home. There was nothing about the dilapidated buildings or littered yard to bespeak the activities of family life. The brooding silence of the plains was emphasized here, became an unpleasant, almost uncanny, gloom and desolation. Later, after meeting Plenty Coups, I understood. It is the home of a tired old man who is waiting, as patiently as may be, for the Great Spirit Chief to call him to the Happy Hunting Ground where dimmed eyes will become bright once more and shaky warped legs straight and strong. For him life's energies are sapped, life's activities stopped.

Inexpressibly disappointed, we lingered on the porch, and presently a white dog came ambling around the house, wagging his tail in cordial welcome, the chief's closest companion, we were to learn. Instantly my questing hand went probing at the dog's ribs. I found them comfortably padded with fat. I was astonished and delighted, for almost every Indian writer has remarked concerning the red man's starved dogs. Of other tribes I cannot speak with authority, but I do know that a Crow would suffer hunger in order to feed a canine friend. In the heart of the Crow is a beautiful tenderness for all small or dependent creatures—horses, children, dogs.

But the dog, though eyes and tail were speaking to us eloquently, had no words in which to convey the whereabouts of his master. Disconsolately we turned away from the deserted house and followed the road that wound on through Pryor Valley to Pryor Creek.

Though the valley is fertile and holds vast possibilities for the progressive farmer, it reveals no hints of prosperity. Here and there is a small field of wheat, fenced pastures rich in grass and running water given over to a grazing horse or two, occasionally a log cabin, windows stuffed with rags or boarded over—no flower gardens, few vegetable gardens, few chickens or pigs or cows, few pieces of farm machinery—the land of a wild people who have not yet learned how to clutch successfully at civilization's weapons.

At the side of the high narrow trail that is the abandoned roadbed of the Burlington Road are methodically arranged rows of stones, marking the graves of workmen who had fallen victims to the smallpox epidemic more than fifty years ago. Neither names nor dates were inscribed. One fancies them young men, hot blood coursing fast, searching for adventure in the West and finding instead oblivion under little heaps of stones. They had joined the vanguard of that civilization that must take its toll in suffering and death.

The whole of Pryor Valley is pregnant with the unwritten history of venturesome men. Even today, streaking across prairie grass, are many parallel lines of yellow flowers. They define the deep ruts made long years ago by sheep wagons and the pioneers' prairie schooners. You may see distinct circles, like man-made flower beds. Once a buffalo wallowed there, snooting deep into pleasantly cool mud as he turned round and round. On high peaks are still traces of Indian wolves who sent blanket signals or smoke signals to wolves on other peaks often thirty miles away. And at the foot of Red Rock Cliff and across Pryor Creek, opposite the mouth of a cañon running west are mounds, two large ones and many smaller, covered with stones and overgrown with greasewood. They are the graves of which Pretty Eagle spoke. They mark the site of a battle fought three hundred and fifty years ago when the Crows, under Rolling Thunder, held their land against the combined forces of all enemy tribes.

Hungry though we were, impatient to build a camp fire on the banks of Pryor and boil coffee and fry bacon, we took time this Sunday morning in the fall of 1931 to add a stone to the mounds in commemoration of a brave people.

On our return later in the day we stopped again at the home of Plenty Coups, and again we were received delightedly by the lonely white dog. As we were about to turn away a young Crow rode up the lane. Dr. Allen asked him in sign language where we could find the chief. He told us what we should have known all along, that Plenty Coups and his people had gone to Billings to attend the Fair.

I tugged at Dr. Allen's coat sleeve. "Ask him," I whispered, "if he has the key to the house. Ask him if he will show us inside."

Dr. Allen's hands made rapid gestures, mysterious to the uninitiated but evidently quite intelligible to the Indian, for he nodded and smiled and flung open the door to admit us into the domain of the last great chief of the Crows.

Fairly quivering with excited curiosity and reverence I stepped across the threshold into the home of a distinguished ruler of a nation. Home! One wonders if the old man whose heart is still the wild heart of the boy A-Leek-Chea-Ahoosh, whose cradle was the boughs of trees, whose boyhood home was a tepee of buffalo skins, has ever been able to make of this log house, built after the manner of the white man's tepee, a veritable home.

Dark log walls, rough, knotted, bare floors, a battered table, a few hard straight-backed chairs, a kitchen cabinet, and, at the window, dusty strings of lace curtains—everything uncomfortable, gloomy, unbeautiful. Nothing anywhere to lend grace to the sordid business of existence.

On the kitchen cabinet were some groceries, an unopened can of coffee, a sack of sugar, a package of cinnamon and a bottle of vanilla extract. Back of the stove—and somehow this to me seemed pathetic—were hung several dainty pale green enameled kettles. Those delicately tinted cooking utensils, together with the dust-grayed wisps of lace at the windows, epitomized the red man's sole inadequate gesture toward his white brother's cult of beauty.

Yet, in former days, the tepees of young Indian women were made beautiful with fruits of their handiwork.

From the center room, the kitchen, we entered a large room running across the front of the house, doubtless the living-room, but offering no bait anywhere to snuggle down comfortably with book or dreams. All was bleak, dingy, disorderly. Again bare time-darkened board floor; bare log walls; at the windows, dust-stiffened streamers of torn lace. No chairs. Two cheap iron beds covered with gray blankets. In one corner a stairway leading to the second floor. And it is said the chief boasts with inordinately childish glee that he has the only two-story house in Pryor Valley, never considering how meet it is that the domicile of a sovereign tower above the humbler dwellings of his subjects. For, though a Crow chief has his pride, that pride does not permit him superior material prosperity while his people suffer want. A chief is usually the poorest of the tribe, for one of the duties of his high position is to share with everyone in need.

A cement fireplace took up one end of the room. On its mantle were stubs of candles, a kerosene lamp, a flashlight, a child's legless rag doll, a pair of spurs. On the floor were saddles, bridles, a red plaid mackinaw, a pair of boots. In an opposite corner stood a tub and washboard, a child's expensive velocipede, and another doll.

One arresting touch of beauty we did see. On

the wall, in a massive gilt frame, hung an enlarged photograph of a Crow boy. The lad, presumably about sixteen, was dressed in Indian costume of royal white. He stood erect, proud, with the bearing of a haughty young prince. But it was the extraordinary loveliness of the face that haunted us— handsome, but more than that—the face of a patrician, with firmly molded lips and dark eyes that flashed their fearless challenge to life. The face of a youth—intelligent, sensitive, spiritual—who must inevitably grow into splendid manhood. That he was not the son of Plenty Coups we knew, for the chief has no children. Since the death of his own two babies the tender lonely heart has fathered all the children of his people. We inquired of our Indian guide the name of the boy, but he shook his head and directed us into the third room.

It was a bedroom. In it were two gray-blanketed beds with a cheap oak chiffonier between. A strip of lace as dingy as the curtains adorned the top of the bureau. On it, leaning against a kerosene lamp, was an old photograph of a group of Crow braves—Dr. Allen recognized among them Pretty Eagle, Iron Bull, Bell Rock, and Plenty Coups.

For a long time I studied the pictured face of the most famous of all Indian chiefs, taken when the man was in his prime. A stern face, yet also kind. Nobility was stamped upon it, and determination and a divine patience. I thought of A-Leek-

Chea-Ahoosh, the gay, harum-scarum lad, full of
life, ready for any prank that spelled fun—A-Leek-
Chea-Ahoosh the youth, hungry for adventure,
into whose ears birds and rustling trees and all small
woods creatures were beginning to whisper en-
trancing mysteries of romance; then A-Leek-Chea-
Ahoosh become Plenty Coups, sobered, a chief, the
greatest of all chiefs, having at heart the best good
for his people, often pitting his shrewd mind
against the ablest diplomats in Washington, fighting for his people a tongue battle of diplomacy, and
winning sometimes; Plenty Coups, a wise, just, pru-
dent man to whom, more and more in later years,
both palefaces and reds turned for counsel and aid;
and now Plenty Coups at eighty-three, still a chief,
still guiding his people, preparing them for the
time soon to come when they must stand alone, in-
stilling into their hearts something of his own
philosophic acceptance of the inevitable, even while
his thoughts turn back to happier days when buffalo roamed the plains and the Indian was ruler
of his destiny.

On the chiffonier, beside the photographed
group, we saw a bottle of eyewash. It brought the
sting to my throat—that futile little bottle of
liquid for eyes hopelessly dimmed. Never until the
Great Spirit Chief calls Plenty Coups across the
Slippery Log will he be able to see again clearly.

That he will cross that precarious log and enter
the Happy Hunting Ground there can be no doubt,

for he has lived up to the best within him. If his moral code has not been our code, neither has ours been his. He has hated his enemies and fought them fearlessly. He has loved his friends and remained true to them in heart and deed. He has been compassionate to all helpless creatures. His intensive worship of the mountain's beauty has prohibited any pettiness of soul. And now, these last days as he sits out his days in cheerless rooms reliving the mad adventures of youth he is biding his time, and his heart sings and he knows no fear.

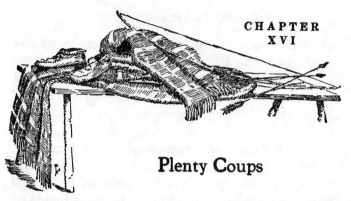

Plenty Coups

THE DAY following our visit to Chief Plenty Coups' home was the opening day of the Midland Empire Fair. Excitement was in the air. You sniffed it in with every breath and felt it coursing through your veins and went heady with its fever. The intoxication of crowds and noise and flags and balloons and extra traffic cops and bands and cowboys seized you.

Upstairs in Dr. Allen's office where we sat waiting for a visit from Chief Plenty Coups there seeped to us only a tempered hum of all the hilarity below. The chief had promised to visit us that morning to renew his friendship with his white brother, White Eagle, and to hear what we had written concerning his people and his life.

Hitherto I had seen him only at a distance as he rode in parades, resplendent in war costume, wearing proudly his gorgeous headdress with its upright painted eagle feathers that bespeak his rank as unmistakably as the bars on an army officer's sleeve. I rejoiced at this rare opportunity of meeting the great chieftain, talking to him, drawing as near as might be to the heart of him.

Ten o'clock, the time set for our appointment! Five after ten— Supposing he did not come! Supposing he had forgotten or given his word carelessly!

Then, before my unreasonable impatience became unendurable, Simon Bull-tail entered the office to say that the elevator was out of order and that the chief could not climb the three flights of stairs without help.

So Dr. Allen went down and I waited, tingling with a curious complexity of emotions. I was about to interview an illustrious personage, the most famous chief of a people clothed in mystery. Presently I heard footsteps along the hall, very slow, then in the doorway appeared Dr. Allen and Simon Bull-tail, supporting between them a little old man, bent, frail, breathing asthmatically, shuffling along on warped legs, in his cheap, ill-fitting "store" suit the most unpicturesque figure imaginable. He is almost blind. His mouth is shrunken over toothless gums. Two scant braids of gray hair hang to his shoulders. After the slightest exertion he breathes heavily. When he speaks his voice is but a rasping whisper.

And this was Plenty Coups, the Chief! A-Leek-Chea-Ahoosh, the fiery, courageous, ambitious lad!

As Simon Bull-tail introduced us and I stood to receive him and saw the two shaking bony hands go groping through the air I extended my own hand gratefully, for this man is not ordinary; it is only the hideous prank of Time that has made him appear so.

I said to the interpreter, Simon Bull-tail, "Tell Chief Plenty Coups I deem it an honor to meet the greatest chief of all Indian tribes."

When the interpreter repeated my words Plenty Coups smiled with the gracious dignity that never questions the homage due his rank. He spoke in his husky whisper and Simon Bull-tail translated:

"Chief Plenty Coups says he is old and very tired. He is blind. It hurts him to talk. He says palefaces annoy him with visits of curiosity. He says he has come here this morning only because he remembers the days when he and White Eagle hunted buffaloes on the plains, and their hearts sang songs of youth. He says he will talk to you because White Eagle is his friend."

They led him to a davenport and seated him between Simon Bull-tail and me. He spoke again.

"He wishes to apologize because we were ten minutes late. He wishes you to know that it is because the taxi kept us waiting."

I assured him apologies were unnecessary. I might have told him it is not the custom of palefaces to be so punctiliously courteous in keeping appointments.

The chief spoke again: "Plenty Coups wishes to know if it will annoy you if he smokes?"

While Simon Bull-tail lit a cigarette and handed it to the chief of a race whom we are pleased to term "savages," I tried to recall the exact words in which Burke defines civilization:

"Our manners, our civilization, and all the good things connected with manners and civilization, in this European world of ours, depended upon two principles—the spirit of a gentleman and the spirit of religion."

We sat for a moment silent. I knew the two copper-skinned gentlemen were waiting with patient courtesy for my questions. But how begin? With what magic words draw from the living heart within the little mummied figure all the glories of the past?

"I should like to know," I ventured, "what Plenty Coups desires for his young men now that the day of the warrior is gone. Since they can never become great chiefs by deeds of daring as he has done what future does he see for them?"

Plenty Coups was slow with his replies, pondering each question before he spoke.

"I want them," he said at last in his strained voice, "to be good boys. I want them to go to school and become well educated. Then I want them to come back home on the reservation and work their land. They must have good houses, good teams, and work very hard. They must not use whiskey or that other very bad stuff that pale-faces sell to our boys."

"Do you mean opium?"

"No, we call it 'peurtie.' Very bad stuff, like opium."

(Plenty Coups referred to the peyote bean, the dried crown of a cactus sold on the reservation at four or five dollars a thousand. The brew from three or four beans produces drug intoxication similar to that produced by opium. Peyote has the doubtful merit of being cheaper than whiskey and easier to get.)

"It makes our boys see visions," the chief explained, gravely, "but not good visions. They call it 'religion,' but it's not religion."

I marveled: "So Indian parents have their anxieties grieving over willful youth caught in the trap of modernism!"

"Is Plenty Coups sorry," I inquired aloud, "that the white man's civilization has spoiled the buffalo range?"

"Yes," he answered, "nothing the white man has given can make up for the happy life when vast plains were unfenced. Then we never worried, for then our hunters brought in plenty hides and meat and our women and children were never hungry or cold. Then our young men were so busy all day long they didn't need whiskey or 'peurtie' for visions. White man kill all buffalo. Take all land. Deer gone, buffalo gone, mountain sheep gone. Now no more game. Sometimes my people hungry. I feel pretty bad about that."

A statement of Shield's came to my mind.

"The Indian has a remarkable faculty of adapting himself to his environment, whatever that may be. He can always find something to eat, something to make fuel of, something to wear."

"Why doesn't the educated Indian adapt himself to white man's ways?" I queried. "Why doesn't he live in cities and make his living as a doctor or merchant or dentist?"

Plenty Coups' words came slowly, hesitantly, as though he were debating the one right way in which to convey his thought.

"Some boys," he said, finally, "like to do that. They become educated, they try to be doctors. But white people don't much like them. White people don't much like Indians."

To that I could think of no fitting reply for I know that against the complexities of white man's civilization the Indian boy has little chance. And the belief, whether well founded or not, that "white people don't much like Indians," shortens his attempted stride upward.

I suggested that Plenty Coups tell us something of his strong medicine and he gave us this story:

"When I was sixteen years old I went up onto Bear Tooth Mountains. I went alone and climbed to the highest point. I stayed up there four days without food or water. The days were very hot and the nights were very cold. I waited and watched and nothing came to me. Then, when I was very weak and suffered from hunger and thirst

so I could not walk any more I lay down on a rock
and gazed up into the Blue. And soon, while I
looked, many eagles—maybe so ten, maybe so
twenty—flew above me and gave me medicine—
strong medicine—you know?"

He paused to interrogate me with a glance,
wondering if I really understood his allusion to
"strong medicine."

When I nodded he went on: "Then I was pretty
weak. I think I never get home. I think I'm going
to die. But the eagles took care of me. They carried me home, back down to my mother's tepee."

The faces of the two Indians were very earnest,
very grave. They were speaking now, reverently,
of matters sacred to them. Simon Bull-tail volun-
teered: "And even now, when Plenty Coups goes
walking or riding out across the plains, eagles fly
over his head. When he sings, then an eagle flies
over his head."

The face of the old chief was becoming animated with memories. He forgot that it hurt him
to talk. He hurried on: "And while I slept up
there, when the eagles came to me, they gave me
a song to sing and the words of the song are these:

> 'Give me nice feathers
> And I will do something nice for you.
> For then you will live long,
> And you will live good,
> With many horses.' "

The chief attempted, in his husky whisper, to croon the melody for us. Just then, up from the noisy street the music of the band was wafted to us. The face of Plenty Coups lit up. He smiled and swayed to the rhythm, beating time with his hands.

"Do you like music?" I asked.

"Yes," he said, "the heart of the red man always sings when he hears music, whether it is the song of pines or of running water or of our tom-toms, or of the white man's band.

"Another time," he continued, "I went up onto the mountains and stayed there four days. That time, too, I became pretty weak and thought I was going to die. Then from above, from the Blue, I saw a white man coming down to me, and he gave me medicine and took care of me and he has taken care of me ever since."

"Is that why you have always been a friend to the white man and have called him 'brother'? Is that why your people fought with the white man instead of against him?"

"Yes, and that's why I've lived so long and been so happy. Because the eagle and the white man have been my strong medicine. I have been frightened lots of times but I don't get killed. The white man came from above and told me to do this or that and I have done it and that's why I have lived so long."

"Do you think," I suggested, "that the Great Spirit sent the eagle and the white man down to you from the Blue?"

He gave thought to my question. "No," he said, frowning in puzzled fashion, "no, we don't believe that. It is not the Great Spirit that sends those visions down to us, but they come to give us strong medicine so we can be brave to fight our enemies. And we believe if we are good—if we never lie or cheat—then, when we die our souls go some place and live like they did on earth."

I recalled the story of the old Crow woman who, knowing she was soon to die, begged that she be taught some new pattern of quilt making so she could resume her fancy work after she had crossed the Slippery Log and landed safe in the Happy Hunting Ground.

As we sat silent, waiting for the spirit to move Plenty Coups to speech, I looked down at him. He was huddled close to the broad-shouldered Simon Bull-tail, appearing in contrast grotesquely feeble and shriveled—the mere shell of that which had once been a vigorous man, full of enthusiasm and confidence and courage.

He is facing the common tragedy of old age bravely, and along with it another, the threatened tragedy of the extinction of a proud and gallant race. He peers far into the future and what he sees does not yield him happiness.

A-Leek-Chea-Ahoosh, eighty years ago, learning from his older brother to walk, ride, swim, shoot with bow and arrow. A-Leek-Chea-Ahoosh, the determined lad, studying the motions of frog

and beaver so he could win in the swimming race
and be—not as good as the best—but the best.
A-Leek-Chea-Ahoosh lying under the trees at night
alone, battling against his first deep grief, the death
of his beloved brother at the hands of the Sioux.
A-Leek-Chea-Ahoosh borne along on an avalanche
of eventful years, years etched against eternity by
his visions on the mountain top, by his first coup,
his first romance, the death of Flying Bird. Pur-
poseful years rushing him upward toward his goal,
from runner to wolf, to headman, to subchief under
Pretty Eagle, and to chief, and then, as a signal
mark of trust from the White Father in Washington, chief of all the tribes of the Northwest.

From time to time honors have come to him.
Once a vast and enthusiastic throng gathered to
cheer him as he rode in state along the streets of
New York. Once he stood with representatives of
rulers of all nations to witness the unveiling of the
monument to the Unknown Soldier. Upon that
occasion he addressed the multitude in words so
apt, so forceful, that critics deemed his speech a
classic, comparable in its beauty of literary form
and thought to the Gettysburg address.

But all that is past, and now a weary old man
waits in perpetual darkness for the call of the
Great Spirit Chief, and as he waits he relives, not
the pomp and glory of later years, but those days
of his joyous, carefree youth.

His earlier reluctance to talk had quite vanished.

Under the spell of memories as he sat on the davenport in Dr. Allen's office, head and hands keeping
time to the band music, he sang for us songs his
mother had crooned to him nights as he was drows-
ing off to sleep.

> *"Every day go out to fight the enemy.*
> *Every day be very strong and brave.*
> *Be fleet of foot*
> *And sure with bow and arrow,*
> *Make the enemy run.*
>
> *"Got to be a warrior!*
> *Got to be a man!*
> *Got to be a strong man*
> *And brave!"*

The old chief whispered something to Simon
Bull-tail and they both laughed.

"He is going to tell you about the 'Magpie
Caper.'"

It is a favorite story of his. He tells it over
and over to any one who will listen.

"Once," he began, "when I was a boy about
ten years old the hunters had brought in to camp
many fat buffalo and for many days the women
were busy tanning hides, making moccasins and
robes—both body and tepee robes. And they cut
the meat into strips and hung them up on tall poles
to dry. There were many buffalo tongues and
much fat meat in our village, so much that when

snows came none of us need fear hunger. And the women worked from morning to night, gathering roots and berries for pemmican."

Though I could not, of course, understand Plenty Coups' words until they had been interpreted, still, as I watched him while he told the story, saw his eloquent hands pointing to arms, legs, face, and to the two thin braids of hair, I caught the contagion of his mirth and laughed, too, even before I was told the meaning of his words.

"So, one day," he chuckled, "while the women were busy and not watching, after all the meat had been hung up to dry, we boys went down to the creek—lots of boys. We covered ourselves all over with mud—arms, legs, faces, so no one could tell who we were. And we tied our braids up over our ears in two funny horns—like this. Then we crept back to the tepees and stole our mother's meat and ran away with it and hid in the forest. Some of the mothers ran after us but we dodged behind trees and ran faster than they. When we were sure no one could find us we built a fire and cooked our meat and ate it. But every time we looked at each other, our faces all covered with mud and our braids sticking out like little horns, we had to laugh so we could hardly eat.

"Then, when we did get back to our village all the people laughed at us and called us 'magpies' because we stole meat."

As Plenty Coups related that naughty prank of so many snows ago he laughed until tears trickled down his withered cheeks. He had shaken off the years and was a boy again, loving laughter.

"Do you remember," Dr. Allen asked him, "the time we first met, on the banks of the Little Horn?"

"Yes, I do remember. That night our hands clasped in friendship. Our hearts spoke. Since then more than fifty snows have fallen upon our heads and we are still friends."

"And do you remember," Dr. Allen continued, "the time we had a battle with Blackfeet out in Lake Basin and how, coming home, we sang war songs and danced war dances?"

Unsteadily Plenty Coups got to his feet and stood beside Dr. Allen, and, with an affectionate hand on White Eagle's shoulder, did a few steps of the dance. Dr. Allen joined in. Laughing, they sang together: "Hey-ya! Hey-ya! Hey-ya-hey!"

Born in the same year, one in a cabin in Ohio, the other in a tepee in Montana, closely bound by the glamorous years—around them and men like them, fearless, adventurous, the history of the West is written. As they stood there, arms interlocked, three stories up from the clatter of busy streets, they were boys again out on the open plain, with the swift hot blood of youth coursing through their veins.

But then Simon Bull-tail spoke in low tones to his chief and to us apologized gravely: "We must be going. Plenty Coups is to ride in the parade today."

"Does he want to?" I asked.

"Oh, yes! His costume is all ready. He likes that pretty much."

We asked Chief Plenty Coups, before he went, to place his signature at the end of our book so that all who read, both his people and palefaces, might know we had spoken with straight tongue concerning his life and that of the Crows.

"What you have written," he said, "is good. You have written the stories of my boyhood when I was so high—" And he extended his hand measuring the height of a child. "And when I was so high—" With a gesture he added inches to his height. "And when I was so high—just as I told them to White Eagle. The rest he knows. Perhaps when palefaces read they will understand the red man and like him pretty much. At the end of your book I will put my thumb print so all may know the written words have come from my heart to yours."

"But we do not want your thumb print," we protested. "We want your signature—your mark."

He shook his head, visibly saddened by this necessity of denying the wish of a friend.

"But why?" we queried.

And then he explained. "That mark," he told us, soberly, "I never use except when I visit the White Father in Washington."

We began to understand. To him the placing of his mark at the end of treaties between Crows

Chief Plenty Coups and his friend, Dr. Allen. Taken at County Fair in 1900. (Crow village and rimrocks in background.) Photograph by Judge Goddard.

I hereby certify that Plenty Coos made this mark in my presence on September 8th, 1931.

Geo Ryburn

Notary Public for the State of Montana. My commission expires January 17, 1933. (SEAL)

HIS

X

MARK

"Having heard this tale of my people read to me through my interpreter, Simon Bull-tail, I make my mark which I use before the Great White Father in Washington so that those who read the book may know White Eagle and the Little Lady have not spoken with crooked tongue."—Chief Plenty Coups. (See page 301.)

and whites had become a sacred ritual. Of course
we would not urge him further.

"That's all right—" Dr. Allen began.

But Plenty Coups held up an arresting hand.
He had been debating the matter in his mind. "I
will make my mark at the end of your book," he
announced, gravely. "Because your heart has spoken
in this book you have written of the Crows and
because White Eagle asks this of me I will do it."

So, while we watched he sat down at the desk,
drew a clean sheet of paper before him, took up the
pen and made his mark, slowly, with meticulous
care, giving much attention to all the little curves.

"Just so," he informed us, "I make it before
the White Father. It is done. I have spoken. Now
I go."

I followed slowly behind him as he tottered
down the hall supported by Dr. Allen and Simon
Bull-tail.

He reached the head of the flight of steps and
began the descent, breathing hard, leaning heavily
upon the two strong arms. A man who had started
down stood back to make way for the old chief.

"Is that Plenty Coups?" he inquired.

When I told him that it was he shook his head
with reverent pity. And then the stranger voiced
the tribute that is in the hearts of all who have had
the privilege of knowing, if ever so little, the greatest Indian chief of all time.

"I knew Plenty Coups," he said, "forty years ago. Then he was at his best. Then there was that something in his face—a fineness, a strength, a nobility, that one doesn't see in the faces of many men. There was something in his face that explained why he had become chief."

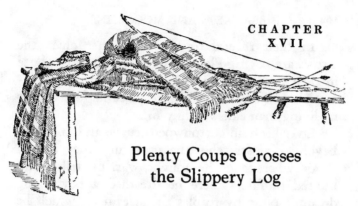

Plenty Coups Crosses
the Slippery Log

ON THE third day of March, 1932, Plenty Coups, chief of all the tribes of the Northwest, last chief of the Crows, died. A long life of service both to his country and to the people of his own race came to an end on that bleak wintry day when the weary old body was laid to rest back of his log house in the grove of trees his own hands had planted in the morning of his youth.

Never again will he sit on sunny days on the veranda of his house, dog close by, smoking, peering with sightless eyes toward the mountains he loved, reliving those glamorous years when he and the West were young. Never again will he, resplendent in warrior costume, head the procession of his people at the Fairs. We shall miss him, but those who knew him best and therefore loved him most cannot grieve, for he was a Jesus man, and we are assured he crossed the Slippery Log safely and entered into the Happy Hunting Ground somewhere up in the vast Blue, where dim eyes are made to see and bent backs become straight.

In their refusal to choose another chief the Crows are paying Plenty Coups the highest tribute in their power, a fine gesture, indeed, that proclamation to the world that the place he left vacant no living man can worthily fill.

Over his head cottonwoods rustle and shimmer. Beyond him stretches the peaceful valley of the Pryor where once he fought warring tribes and hunted buffalo, where he dreamed a boy's long dreams. Near by ripples the stream on which he and his brother launched their bull-boat. Beyond and above loom the mountains, epitome always to him of beauty and refuge and God.

Long ago, spurred on by youth's shining faith, he climbed those mountains seeking visions and, by means of them, his God. Then he saw through a glass darkly, but now, we trust, face to face.